THE MEDITATIONS OF MARCUS AURELIUS

THE MEDITATIONS OF MARCUS AURELIUS

MARCUS AURELIUS

Translated from the Greek
BY JEREMY COLLIER

Revised, with an Introduction and Notes
BY ALICE ZIMMERN.

GYAN

Published by

GYAN

Gyan Publishing House
5, Ansari Road
Daryaganj, New Delhi-110002
Phone: 011-47034999, 9811692060
E-mail: books@gyanbooks.com

Distribution Network
gyanbooks.com
India, USA, Canada, UK, Australia

ISBN: 978-93-6208-813-0 (PB)
First Published, 1887

2nd Impression 2024

Printed at: Gyan Press, Delhi.

THE MEDITATIONS OF MARCUS AURELIUS
Author: MARCUS AURELIUS, Translator: JEREMY COLLIER,
Introduction: ALICE ZIMMERN

THE MEDITATIONS OF MARCUS AURELIUS

THE

MEDITATIONS

OF

MARCUS AURELIUS

Translated from the Greek

BY JEREMY COLLIER

Revised, with an Introduction and Notes

BY ALICE ZIMMERN.

LONDON
WALTER SCOTT, 24 WARWICK LANE
PATERNOSTER ROW
1887

CONTENTS.

MARCUS AURELIUS.

"UNTIL philosophers are kings, and the princes of this world have the spirit and power of philosophy, and political greatness and wisdom meet in one, cities will never cease from ill—no, nor the human race, as I believe—and then only will our state have a possibility of life, and see the light of day." "The truth is, that the state in which the rulers are most reluctant to govern is best and most quietly governed, and the state in which they are most willing is the worst."

Thus writes Plato in his Republic, laying down the conditions, which even to him appear impossible, under which a state may be wisely governed. The ruler must be a philosopher as well as a king; and he must govern unwillingly, because he loves philosophy better than dominion. Once in the history of the world these conditions were fulfilled: in Marcus Aurelius we find the philosopher king, the ruler who preferred the solitude of the student to the splendour of the palace, the soldier who loved the arts of peace better than the glory of war. It is with no small interest that we turn to the records of history to see what was the outward life led by this king; but even more willingly do we open the precious record of his own thoughts, which reveal to us the inner life of the philosopher.

Marcus Aurelius Antoninus was the adopted son of the Emperor Antoninus Pius, who died in 161 A.D. He had been brought up with the utmost care by his adoptive father, and received the best instruction in poetry and rhetoric, at that time the staples of a liberal education. But his favourite study was philosophy, and when only eleven years old he assumed the philosophers' simple dress, adopted their mode of life; and finding that his inclination was chiefly towards Stoicism, he attached himself to this—the strictest of the philosophic schools. A discipline of monastic severity, that bade its followers disregard all bodily comfort, all that is commonly called pleasure, and care for nought but virtue, was indeed a strange training for one destined for the imperial purple, and it hardly appeared to be a fitting preparation for the cares of what was then the one great Empire of the world. True, the Stoics loved to call themselves citizens of the world, and to inculcate that cosmopolitanism that is broader and nobler than mere patriotism; but while they maintained in theory that the wise man should take part in politics, in practice there was always something in the existing state of things which made his doing so unadvisable. But Marcus Aurelius could not choose his own lot. Destined for the throne already by the Emperor Hadrian, associated in the empire even in his adoptive father's lifetime, he could but accept his lot, and in striving to practise the noble principles he had learnt, pay to his Stoic teachers the truest tribute.

His was a troubled reign. The Roman Empire, which in the vigorous days of the Republic had been gradually but surely extending its boundaries, had been consolidated, and newly administered by Julius Cæsar and Augustus. On the death of the latter it extended from the Atlantic on the west to the Armenian mountains and Arabian deserts on the east. On the south the African deserts had alone stopped the conquering arms, while on the north a line of natural boundaries was traced by the English Channel, Rhine, Danube, Black Sea, and Mount Caucasus. Warned by the ill-success that attended the later campaigns of his generals on the Lower Rhine, Augustus had cautioned his successors to aim at preserving rather than increasing their dominions. Thus it came about, that between the years 14 and 161 A.D., when Marcus Aurelius succeeded to the throne, only two fresh conquests had been made; Britain, a source of more trouble than profit to the empire, and Dacia, conquered by Trajan in 106 A.D.

Natural boundaries and Roman legions kept peace and security for many years within the circle of Roman dominion. But there were two weak points on these borders. On the north the hardy German tribes on the Danube and Upper Rhine, themselves hard pressed by Slavonian intruders from Russia, threatened to invade the Roman dominion; on the east the "insolent Parthian," long the terror of the Roman arms, was a constant source of trouble and danger. The peace-loving Marcus Aurelius was obliged to cope with both these enemies. The arms, or rather the army, of the insolent and profligate Lucius Verus for a time subdued the Parthians, but no lasting peace was destined Marcus Aurelius. He himself conducted the campaigns on the Danube, and again and again beat back the northern enemy in wars, of which the chief interest to us now consists in the scant notes in the *Meditations*—"This among the Quadi," "this at Carmuntum," showing how these precious records of a pure and serene soul were composed amid the storms of battle and the elation of victory. Nor were his troubles confined to foreign wars. The plague, imported from the East, ravaged Italy, though it did the state good service in carrying off Lucius Verus, Marcus's adoptive brother, whom, in obedience to the wishes of Antoninus, he had associated with himself in the empire. There were famines too in the land, with which the Emperor tried to cope by schemes of carefully-organised charity. And, lastly, Avidius Cassius, one of his most trusted and ablest generals, revolted in Syria, and tried to obtain for himself the empire, deeming it an easy matter to overcome a master who was so full of generosity and compassion that he could only inspire contempt in the mind of the unphilosophic soldier. The revolt was soon put down, but the leader was killed by one of his own officers. The Emperor expressed only his regret that he should have been thus deprived of the luxury of forgiveness, and he carefully destroyed all documents that could implicate any others in the revolt. Thus in all the trials of his life his philosophy inspired noble action, and he might worthily be added to the short list of those whom the Stoics acknowledged as really good and great.

Amid these records of gentleness and forbearance it seems strange to read that Marcus Aurelius permitted a cruel persecution of the Christians. Among the victims of this reign were Justin Martyr and Polycarp, and numbers suffered in a general persecution of the churches at Lyons and Vienne. It must not, however, be forgotten that the persecution was political rather than religious. Of the true teaching of Christianity Marcus Aurelius knew little and cared less; but its followers, in refusing to acknowledge a religion which included the

Emperors among its deities, became rebels against the existing order of things, and therein culpable. Of the old sincere belief in the gods of Rome but little could survive in a state where the vote of the Senate had the power to add a new divinity to the already bewildering list. So much the more important were the outward forms, now that the actual belief was gone, and the bond between Church and State grew even closer, now that the Church could no longer stand alone. Of the various systems of philosophy at that time fashionable at Rome, all but the Epicurean could readily embody the creed of the old religion, and by treating the names of gods and heroes as mere symbols, they contrived to combine outward conformity with inner enlightenment. Not so the Christians. In their eyes the whole system of idolatry was accursed. A silent protest was insufficient. It was not enough to refrain from sacrifice themselves; in public and in private, in season and out of season, they exhorted others to do the like; not content with leaving the statues of the gods unhonoured, they would throw them from their pedestals, or insult them in the presence of the faithful. What wonder that the Romans looked on them with suspicion and hatred, and added to their real offences the pretended ones of eating human flesh and indulging in all manner of immorality. In our own more enlightened day we know what strange reports gather round any sect or school that happens to be unfashionable or unpopular. What wonder, then, that the secret meetings of the Christians should have given rise to strange rumours, and that the persecutions "were the expression of a feeling with which a modern state might regard a set of men who were at once Mormons and Nihilists."* Add to this that the Christians often actually provoked

* F. Myer's *Classical Essays.*

persecution, and we cease to wonder, though we cannot but regret, that Marcus Aurelius, in simply allowing the law to take its course, should have failed to give an example of that perfect toleration to which Christianity itself has never yet attained. Let us be content to call him, with Farrar, "the noblest of Pagan Emperors," and sorrowfully acknowledge that we must seek in vain for a Christian monarch to place beside him. Wars and troubles attended Marcus Aurelius to the very end of his days. In 177 A.D. fresh wars called him to the north. A presentiment seemed to tell his friends at Rome that they should not see him again, and they begged him to address them his farewell admonitions. There is nothing more striking in the whole of Aurelius' career than this picture of the great general discoursing for three days before his departure for the wars on the deep questions of philosophy. This was indeed the last time he was seen at Rome. Worn out by anxiety and fatigue, after once more winning victory for the Roman arms, he died, in Pannonia, on March 17th, 180 A.D., mourned with a note of such true sorrow as never before or again was raised at the death of an Emperor.

It is time to inquire into the nature of that philosophy which was capable of exercising an influence so distinctly practical; yet, when we consider its teaching as laid down by its founders, its distinct materialism and impracticable ethics afford little suggestion of such fruits as it was destined to bear in the Roman world.

The Stoic school was founded by Zeno at Athens about 290 B.C. At this time Greek philosophy, which, under Socrates, Plato, and Aristotle, had lived through a short period of idealism, was returning to its naturally materialistic groove, and the founders of new systems looked back to the pre-Socratic physicists for some theory of the universe on which they might base their own. Metaphysical speculation had ceased to charm; it was practical ethics, a rule of life and conduct, that philosophy now desired to supply; and though these later schools based ethics on natural science, they were content to go back to the investigators of old for a system, instead of devoting themselves on their own account to scientific research. The two most important schools at this epoch were the Stoic and Epicurean; and while the latter sought in the atomic theory of Democritus an explanation of the universe, the former reverted to the "perpetual flux," the eternal, ever-changing fire of Heraclitus.

Before there was a heaven or earth there was a primitive fiery ether. This changes into all the other elements, and yet in its nature ever retains the fiery substratum. First this fiery ether transforms itself into a mass of vapour, then into a watery fluid. Out of this are developed the four elements as we know them: water, and solid earth, and atmospheric air, and lastly consuming, destructive fire, which is distinct from the everlasting ether. Fire and air are active elements; water and earth, passive. The creation begins to assume its present form with earth; dry earth, by reason of its weight, takes up a position at the centre of the universe, around it gather the waters, above both is the expanse of air, while fire and ether complete the whole, ever circling round the other elements which are at rest. The stars are fiery masses firmly embedded in ether, and nourished by the exhalations of terrestrial vapours. But they are also living beings, since they are formed out of living, animating fire, and they may thus be regarded as inferior or visible gods. "The sun and the celestial deities, too, have their business assigned," says Marcus Aurelius.

The world is faultless, say the Stoics, and must therefore have been produced by an intelligent artificer. Hence the highest reason is immanent in the world, and must be regarded as self-conscious and personal. For has it not created man, who is self-conscious and personal, and can the created be greater than the creator? And yet, paradoxical as it may seem, the Stoic god is not a person, but is the fiery ether that pervades all things. This fiery substratum of all matter is its soul; the soul of the universe, which holds together all things in one fixed law, is God himself. In one aspect the Deity is but a fiery air-current; in another he is Zeus, the intelligent, almost personal lord of the universe. Both these aspects may be found in Marcus Aurelius; but in him the simpler ethical teaching, the gentle exhortation to a virtuous life, predominate over subtle speculation on the origin of things, and be speaks of God in language that suggests vividly to us the omnipotent, omniscient, Deity of Monotheism.

The Stoics traced back all things to formless matter and the informing, animating ether. Matter was in its nature eternal, since the underlying fire was imperishable; but all things were being gradually consumed, and at the end of a fixed period there would be a general conflagration, when all things should be reabsorbed into the Deity. Then once more they would be developed afresh, and another cycle begin.

> "The world's great age begins anew,
> The golden days return,
> The earth doth like a snake renew
> Her winter weeds outworn,"

sings Shelley, but the Stoics expected no "brighter Hellas," or "fairer Tempes." The new things should be but as the old; in the new cycle there should be another Socrates, destined to marry another Xanthippe, and meet with the same rough treatment at her hands, and finally to be accused by Anytus and Meletus, and once more utter his glorious defence, and drain the cup of hemlock among his sorrowing disciples.

Some such scheme of the universe was certainly accepted by all the Stoics, but the later teachers, at any rate, attached little importance to it, except in as far as it demonstrated man's intimate connection with the Deity and his fellow-men. They believed that the soul was material, and extended in space. It is the fiery current that is diffused through the body, and holds it together. They regarded it as the guiding or dominant principle, the indestructible divine spark. It is this, the reasoning element, which establishes the relationship between God, the universal reason, and man, to whose lot has fallen a minute share of it; while the brotherhood of Man is maintained in virtue of a kinship, not of flesh and blood, but of mind and reason. "Though we are not just of the same flesh and blood, yet our minds are nearly related." (*Marcus Aurelius*, *Med.* ii. 1.)

Did the Stoics believe in a life after death? It is not easy to decide. They did not, like the Epicureans, fiercely deny it, maintaining that annihilation alone could remove the terrors of death. Undoubtedly the individual soul must at last be absorbed into the universal soul; but whether this happened at once, or not until the next conflagration, was a point on which authorities were not agreed. In any case, the soul must return to the Deity whence it sprang. This relation to the Deity was the fundamental point of Stoic ethics. It follows from the kinship that man's true good must lie in conformity with the Deity. But God and reason are identical. Therefore, life in accordance with reason must be best suited to the constitution of the soul. And such a life must be in accordance with virtue. Hence this is the highest good, and happiness consists in virtue.

Thus the Stoics arrive at their main thesis. Virtue alone is admirable, virtue is absolutely self-sufficient; the good man needs no help from circumstances, neither sickness nor adversity can harm him; he is a king, a god among men. All so-called good, if it be not moral good, is included in the class of "things intermediate," neither good nor bad. Such absolute claims for virtue had never before been made by any school. Aristotle had stipulated for sufficient external advantages to enable a man to devote himself without further care to the life of thought and virtue. The Stoics would permit of no such compromise. Virtue, and virtue only, was what they demanded. The virtuous man might be a slave, a victim to disease, to poverty, might be deprived of all he loved, yet he would remain solely and absolutely happy. Virtue was one and indivisible. Whoever was not virtuous was vicious; there was no middle course. Here was a point in their doctrine which could hardly be made to square with fact. We know too well that men are not divided into virtuous and vicious, but all possess some share of good and evil, and that most men desire what is right, and fail, when they do, from weakness rather than viciousness. The Stoics, who demanded absolute virtue and disregard of externals, had to confess that the wise men were few and the foolish legion; nay, when hard pressed to name their wise men, they would give a remarkable list—Hercules, Odysseus, Socrates, the Cynics Antisthenes and Diogenes; and in the later days of the school, Cato the younger, the only Stoic among the number.

Such a list alone appears to us sufficient condemnation of Stoicism in its earlier forms. Had no further advance been made, Stoicism would be of small interest to us now, but happily it was destined, as Capes remarks in his little handbook on Stoicism, to be "tempered by concessions to common sense." The paradoxes about the wise man had been borrowed from Cynicism, which was regarded by the Stoics as "a counsel of perfection." Diogenes in his tub, bidding Alexander stand out of his sunshine, might excite surprise and wonder; but a movement that should lead a whole community to abandon civilisation and resort to life in tubs would be distinctly retrogressive. In later times Christian hermits have at best saved their own souls, and the exhortations delivered by St. Simeon Stylites from the top of his pillar cannot have influenced the gaping multitude as much as a noble life led in their midst. Without the practical element there would have been no life in Christianity, and Stoicism similarly had to descend from its pedestal, and walk among men.

First of all, the theory of absolute good and evil had to be modified. Virtue was still the only real good, and vice the only real evil; but besides these they now admitted a class of "things to be preferred," and another of "things to be avoided." Among the former might be included health, good repute, and other advantages which had formerly been summarily disposed of as "indifferent." Again, while the impossible wise man still remained the ideal of Stoicism, it was admitted that there might be good men with lofty aims and blameless lives who should yet dwell among men as their fellows. In short, the wide gap between the sage and the fool was now filled up, and as a result the Stoic system was able to find a place for real, existing human beings.

These more practical developments were coincident with its introduction into the Roman world. The Romans were nothing if not practical. A nation of soldiers and lawyers, they had borrowed from Greece her culture, and adapted it to their own needs. So too they borrowed their philosophy. When "conquered Greece led her barbarous conqueror captive," a few of the nobler minds at Rome discovered that there was something at Athens worth carrying off besides the statues. Some would spend a year or two at Athens studying philosophy; others induced the greatest teachers themselves to bring their doctrines to Rome; and in the first century B.C. all the Greek systems were represented in the capital of the world. Among them all Stoicism found most adherents. Its teachings of simplicity, resignation, and calm in the midst of disturbance, found willing listeners among the earnest Republicans, who saw their hopes of liberty gradually fading before the approaching monarchy. Its doctrine that suicide was admissible, even admirable, when circumstances made it no longer possible "to take arms against a sea of troubles," pointed to a mode of escape from the tyranny they could not avert. Thus Cato sought death at his own hands when the Republic perished, and it was Stoic teaching that forbade Brutus and Cassius, though not Stoics themselves, to survive the battle of Philippi.

In the early days of the empire, when corruption and license were at their height, the court evinced deep hatred against the philosophers, more especially the Stoics. The outspoken manner in which they chastised the wickedness of the time may have led to their unpopularity; in any case, there were several decrees of banishment against them, and among the victims at one time was—

"That halting slave, who in Nicopolis
Taught Arrian, when Vespasian's brutal son
Cleared Rome of what most shamed him."

Well might the name of Epictetus be counted among those who cheer the soul in evil days, for where can sweeter resignation or truer piety be found than in such words as these—"Dare to look up to God and say, Deal with me for the future as thou wilt, I am of the same mind as thou art; I am thine: I refuse nothing that pleases thee: lead me where thou wilt: clothe me in any dress thou choosest: is it thy will that I should hold the office of a magistrate, that I should be in the condition of a private man, stay here or be an exile, be poor, be rich? I will make thy defence to men in behalf of all these conditions." These were not empty words, for they found their illustration in the life of the speaker.

In the lame slave Stoic ethics rose to its noblest heights; but it was left to the imperial philosopher, by broadening and humanising its teaching, to give to the world in his *Meditations* "the gospel of those who do not believe in the supernatural."

These *Meditations* were not written as a whole—probably they were never intended for publication; they are simply the Emperor's commonplace book, where he entered his reflections, often quite unconnected, on the things of time and eternity. By this means he seems to have adopted his own counsel of withdrawing into his own mind, there to seek calm and quiet. It is noteworthy that in Marcus Aurelius the claims of natural affection are never disregarded. Book I. is entirely devoted to recording his obligation to his parents, friends, and teachers for the benefit of good training or example. For all those helps and advantages which can be traced to none of these, he simply thanks "the gods," without further discussion or inquiry into their nature. The same loving disposition gives life to the Stoic doctrine of the citizenship of the world. Marcus Aurelius truly finds himself akin to all mankind. "Mankind are under one common law; and if so, they must be fellow-citizens, and belong to the same body politic. From whence it will follow that the whole world is but one commonwealth" (*Med.* iv. 4). "Now a social temper is that which man was principally designed for" (vii. 55). This brotherhood of man will lead us to strive for the common good, and reckon nothing else our own advantage. "That which is not for the interest of the whole swarm is not for the interest of a single bee" (vi. 54). It will lead us also to pity and forgive our enemies. "And since it has fallen to my share to understand the natural beauty of a good action and the deformity of an ill one; since I am satisfied the person disobliging is of kin to me, and though we are not just of the same flesh and blood, yet our minds are nearly related, being both extracted from the Deity, I am convinced that no man can do a real injury, because no man can force me to misbehave myself; nor can I find it in my heart to hate or be angry with one of my own nature and family. For we are all made for mutual assistance, as the feet, the hands, and the eyelids; as the rows of the upper and under teeth" (ii. 1). Marcus Aurelius loves to dwell on the instability and insignificance of all things. "The vast continents of Europe and Asia are but corners of the creation; the ocean is but a drop, and Mount Athos but a grain in respect of the universe, and the present instant of time but a point to the extent of eternity. These things have all of them little, changeable, and transitory beings" (vi. 36). We should accustom ourselves to watch the eternal course of destruction, and realise that the universe itself sustains no harm. The death of one thing is the birth of another. "The universal nature works the universal matter like wax. Now, for the purpose, it is a horse; soon after you will have it melted down and run it into the figure of a tree; then a man, then something else. And it is but a little while that it is fixed in one species. Now a trunk feels no more pain by being knocked in pieces than when it was first put together" (vii. 23). "Death and generation are both mysteries of nature, and somewhat resemble each other; for the first does but dissolve those elements the latter had combined" (iv. 5). Amid all this change the only true good is philosophy, which teaches us to keep our guiding principles pure and untainted by bodily impressions. "Toss me into what climate or state you please. For all that, I will keep my divine part content if it but exist and act in accordance with its nature" (viii. 45). Nothing external can influence us, unless we pronounce it good or evil. This is in accordance with the Stoic doctrine, that all sensations make a material impression on the soul; but it is left to the reasoning or guiding principle to decide whether they are true or false, good or evil. "Hold in honour your opinionative faculty, for this alone is able to prevent any opinion from originating in your guiding principle that is contrary to nature or the proper constitution of a rational creature" (iii. 9.) "Do not suppose you are hurt, and your complaint ceases; cease your complaint, and you are not hurt" (iv. 7), writes the Emperor, using, as he so often does, an obscure dogma to point a practical moral.

Such practical teaching abounds in Marcus Aurelius; but he rises to higher flights. How gladly he quotes Antisthenes's comment on the kingly prerogative. "It is a royal thing to be ill-spoken of for good deeds" (vii. 36). How well he satirises the craving for gratitude, so aptly defined by a French writer as the 'usury' we exact for our good deeds. "Some men, when they do you a kindness, at once demand the payment of gratitude from you; others are more modest than this. However, they remember the favour, and look upon you as their debtor in a manner. A third sort shall scarce know what they have done. These are much like a vine, which is satisfied by being fruitful in its kind, and bears a bunch of grapes without expecting any thanks for it. A fleet horse or greyhound do not make a noise when they have done well, nor a bee neither when she has made a little honey. And thus a man that has done a kindness never proclaims it, but does another as soon as he can, just like a vine that bears again the next season. Now we should imitate those who are so obliging as hardly to reflect on their beneficence" (v. 6). And how scathing is this criticism of the affectation of virtue! "How fulsome and hollow does that man look that cries—'I am resolved to deal straightforwardly with you.' Hark you, friend, what need of all this flourish? Let your actions speak; your face ought to vouch for your speech. I would have virtue look out of the eye, no less apparently than love does in the sight of the beloved. I would have honesty and sincerity so incorporated with the constitution that it should be discoverable by the senses" (xi. 15).

Here is another gem that sparkles with especial brightness—"The best way of revenge is not to imitate the injury" (vi. 6).

Very noble is this conception of the true function of prayer—"This man . . . invokes the gods to set him free from some trouble; let it be your petition that your mind may never put you upon such a wish. A third is very devout to prevent the loss of his son. But I would have you pray rather against the fear of losing him. Let this be the rule for your devotions" (ix. 40). To quote from the *Meditations* is a tempting task, but they lie before the reader, and he can make his own choice. We must however briefly inquire how Marcus Aurelius treats those great questions to which each system must find some answer, or else abandon its claims to be a guide through life. The origin of evil is a difficulty that every system has had to meet. It is the first and most obvious argument against the existence of an All-wise Providence. The Stoics boldly faced the difficulty, and denied the facts. The world is perfect, they said; all that seems evil is required for the general good. On this point Marcus Aurelius is perfectly orthodox, but he condemns too curious inquiry. "Does your cucumber taste bitter?—let it alone. Are there brambles in your way?—avoid them then. Thus far you are well. But, then, do not ask, 'What does the world with such things as this?' for a natural philosopher would laugh at you. This expostulation is just as wise as it would be to find fault with a carpenter for having sawdust, or a tailor shreds, in his shop." Epictetus had said: "As a mark is not set up for the purpose of missing it, so neither does the nature of evil exist in the universe;" that is, there is no absolute evil, it is all subordinated to good. So too Marcus Aurelius: "Wickedness generally does no harm to the universe; so too in particular subjects it does no harm to anyone" (viii. 55). At times he points not to the universal law, which he regards as the providence of the universe, but to the existence of gods, who must direct all things for the best. But he never asserts this with any certainty. The alternative is between gods and atoms, between providence and chance; and though Marcus Aurelius pronounces for the former, he desires to show that even under the latter a man may be content. As to the future life, he never speaks with any certainty. The guiding principle of the soul can never perish, since it is a part of the Deity; but whether there is a future self-conscious existence is a question he scarcely touches on. This life is all that concerns us. "Though you were destined to live three thousand, or, if you please, thirty thousand years, yet remember that no man can lose any other life than that which he lives now, neither is he possessed of any other than that which he loses" (ii. 14).

The Stoic Emperor cannot say with our modern poet—

> "What is our failure here but a triumph's evidence
> For the fulness of the days? Have we withered or agonised?
> Why else was the pause prolonged but that singing might issue thence?
> Why rushed the discords in, but that harmony might be prized?"—

but he draws a noble moral from the transitoriness of our being. Not "Let us eat and drink, for to-morrow we die," is the teachings of the *Meditations*, but rather, "Let us use this life well, since we have no other." The consolation for death must be sought in the consciousness of duty done. If we have lived well, we should be content to die, no matter whether our years be many or few. Epicurus bade his followers depart from life as a guest from a banquet satisfied with his entertainment; the Stoics, in sterner language, bid us leave the stage as an actor who has performed his part. "Hark ye, friend; you have been a burgher of this great city. What matter whether you have lived in it but five years or three? If you have observed the laws of the corporation, the length or shortness of the time makes no difference. Where is the hardship, then, if Nature, that planted you here, orders your removal? You cannot say you are sent off by a tyrant or an unjust judge. No; you quit the stage as fairly as a player does that has his discharge from the master of the revels. But I have only gone through three acts, and not held out till the end of the fifth, you say. Well, but in life three acts make the play entire. He that ordered the first scene now gives the sign for shutting up the last. You are neither accountable for one nor the other. Therefore, retire well-satisfied, for he by whom you are dismissed is satisfied also" (xii. 36).

The lovers of Marcus Aurelius have been many, and of every shade of opinion. Long quotes from the preface to Pierron's translation—"A man illustrious in the church, the Cardinal Francis Barberini the elder, nephew of Pope Urban VIII., occupied the last years of his life in translating into his native language the thoughts of the Roman Emperor, in order to diffuse among the faithful the fertilising and vivifying seeds. He dedicated this translation to his soul, in order to make it, as he says, redder than his purple at the sight of the virtues of this Gentile." Montesquieu says of Marcus Aurelius: "On sent en soi-même un plaisir secret lorsqu' on parle de cet empereur; on ne peut lire sa vie sans une espèce d' attendrissement. . . . Tel est l' effet qu'il produit qu' on a meilleure opinion de soi-même parce qu' on a meilleure opinion des hommes."

Matthew Arnold, in his *Essays in Criticism*, points out with his usual clearness the reason of this popularity—"It is remarkable how little of a merely local or temporary character, how little of those *scoriæ* which a reader has to clear away before he gets to the precious ore, how little that even admits of doubt and question, the morality of Marcus Aurelius exhibits." "In general the action Marcus Aurelius prescribes is action which every sound nature must recognise as right, and the motives he assigns are motives which every clear reason must recognise as valid. And so he remains the special friend and comforter of all clear-headed and scrupulous, yet pure and upward-striving souls, in those ages most especially which walk by sight and not by faith, and yet have no open vision. He cannot give such souls, perhaps, all they yearn for, but he gives them much, and what he gives them they can receive."

Perhaps there never was an age that more needed such teaching than our own. On one hand, sectarian hatred and dogmatism almost obscure the great truths common to all mankind; on the other, merciless and destructive criticism, in undermining much that used to be generally accepted, seems at times to threaten even the foundations of truth. Here we may turn, as Renan bids us, to the 'absolute religion' of the *Meditations*—"La religion de Marc Aurèle est la religion absolue, celle qui rèsulte du simple fait d'une haute conscience morale placée en face de l'univers. Elle n' est d' aucune race ni d' aucun pays. Aucune révolution, aucune changement, aucune découverte, ne pourront la changer."

The *Meditations* are chiefly known to English readers in Long's translation, a most scholarly work, and remarkable for its perfect fidelity to the original. Its one defect is a certain lack of vigour, though it must be confessed that the original too is defective in point of style and finish. Before this appeared, the best-known translation was Jeremy Collier's, a book with a charm all its own, in fact, a version far more spirited than the original. Greek scholars must always delight in Long's perfect accuracy, but Collier's work has a value of its own. "Jeremy Collier, too," observes Matthew Arnold, "like Mr. Long, regarded in Marcus Aurelius the living moralist, and not the dead classic; and his warmth of feeling gave to his style an impetuosity and rhythm, which, from Mr. Long's style (I do not blame him on that account) are absent." Long had found fault with Collier's translation as "coarse and vulgar." Mr. Arnold objects;—"Jeremy Collier's real defect as a translator is not his coarseness and vulgarity, but his imperfect acquaintance with Greek."

An attempt is here made to offer to the reader a corrected, though I dare not say a correct, version of Collier's translation. The general scheme of his work has been left unaltered, but gross errors have been corrected, and modern expressions substituted for others that have grown obsolete. In a few cases, where the translator seemed to have entirely misapprehended the meaning, short passages have been re-written. In this work Long's translation and a German version by Cless have afforded me invaluable help, and in some cases I have made use of a very charming, though antiquated, seventeenth century translation by Meric Casaubon. In revising Book IV., I have used Crossley's most helpful Notes. My warm thanks are due to Mr. R. D. Hicks and Mr. E. V. Arnold of Trinity College, Cambridge, and to Mr. R. Garnett of the British Museum, for valuable help in this work and in the correction of proofs.

ALICE ZIMMERN.

BOOK I.

THE EMPEROR MARCUS AURELIUS ANTONINUS:

HIS MEDITATIONS;

OR, DISCOURSES WITH HIMSELF.

BOOK I.

1. THE example of my grandfather Verus gave me a good disposition, not prone to anger.

2. By the recollection of my father's character, I learned to be both modest and manly.

3. As for my mother, she taught me to have regard for religion, to be generous and open-handed, and not only to forbear from doing anybody an ill turn, but not so much as to endure the thought of it. By her likewise I was bred to a plain, inexpensive way of living, very different from the common luxury of the rich.

4. I have to thank my great-grandfather that I did not go to a public school, but had good masters at home, and learnt to know that one ought to spend liberally on such things.

5. From my governor I learned not to join either the green or the blue faction on the race-ground, nor to support the *Parmularius* or *Scutarius* at the gladiators' shows. He taught me also to put my own hand to business upon occasion, to endure hardship and fatigues, and to throw the necessities of nature into a little compass; that I ought not to meddle with other people's business, nor be easy in giving credit to informers.

6. From Diognetus, to shun vain pursuits, not to be led away with the impostures of wizards and soothsayers, who pretend they can discharge evil spirits, and do strange feats by the strength of a charm; not to keep quails for the pit, nor to be eager after any such thing. This Diognetus taught me to bear freedom and plain-dealing in others, and apply myself to philosophy. He also procured me the instruction of Bacchius, Tandasis, and Marcianus. He likewise put me upon improving myself by writing dialogues when I was a boy; prevailed with me to prefer a couch covered with hides to a bed of state; and reconciled me to other like rigours of the Grecian discipline.

7. It was Rusticus that first made me desire to live rightly, and come to a better state; who prevented me from running into the vanity of the sophists, either by writing speculative treatises, haranguing upon moral subjects, or making a fantastical appearance or display of generosity or discipline. This philosopher kept me from yielding to the charms of rhetoric and poetry, from affecting the character of a man of

pleasantry, from wearing my senator's robe in the house, or anything of this kind which looks like conceit and affectation. He taught me to write letters in a plain, unornamental style, like that dated by him from Sinuessa to my mother. By his instructions I was persuaded to be easily reconciled to those who had misbehaved themselves and disobliged me, as soon as they desired reconciliation. And of the same master I learned to read an author carefully. Not to take up with a superficial view, or assent quickly to idle talkers. And, to conclude with him, he gave me his own copy of Epictetus's memoirs.

8. Apollonius taught me to give my mind its due freedom, and disengage it from dependence upon chance, and not to regard, though ever so little, anything uncountenanced by reason. To maintain an equality of temper, even in acute pains, and loss of children, or tedious sickness. His practice was an excellent instance, that a man may be forcible and yet unbend his humour as occasion requires. The heaviness and impertinence of his scholars could seldom rouse his ill-temper. As for his learning, and the peculiar happiness of his manner in teaching, he was so far from being proud of himself upon this score, that one might easily perceive, he thought it one of the least things which belonged to him. This great man let me into the true secret of receiving an obligation, without either lessening myself, or seeming ungrateful to my friend.

9. The philosopher Sextus recommended good-humour to me, and showed me the pattern of a house-

hold governed in a fatherly manner. He also bade me make nature and reason my rule to live by. By his precedent I was instructed to appear with an unaffected gravity, to study the temper and circumstances of my friends in order to oblige them. I saw him bearing with the ignorant and undiscerning, complaisant and obliging to all people, so that his conversation was more charming than flattery; and yet at the same time he was held in the highest reverence by others. Conversing with this philosopher helped me to draw up a true, intelligible, and methodical scheme for life and manners, and never so much as to show the least sign of anger, or any other disturbing thought, but to be perfectly calm and indifferent, yet tender-hearted. However, he let me see in himself that a man might show his good-will significantly enough, without noise and display, and likewise possess great knowledge without vanity and ostentation.

10. Alexander the Grammarian taught me not to be ruggedly critical about words, nor find fault with people for improprieties of phrase or pronunciation, but to set them right by speaking the thing properly myself, and that either by way of answer, assent, or inquiry, or by some such other indirect and suitable correction.

11. Fronto taught me that envy, tricking, and dissimulation are the character and consequences of tyranny; and that those we call patricians have commonly not much fatherly feeling in them.

12. Alexander the Platonist advised me, that without necessity I should never say to anyone, nor write

in a letter, that I am not at leisure, nor make business an excuse to decline frequently the offices of humanity to those we dwell with.

13. I learned of Catulus not to slight a friend for making a remonstrance, though it should happen to be unreasonable, but rather to endeavour to restore him to his natural humour. That, like Domitius and Athenodotus, I should always speak well of those who had the care of my education, and that I should always preserve an hearty affection for my children.

14. I am indebted to Severus for the love I bear to my relations, and towards justice and truth. He likewise made me acquainted with the character and sentiments of Cato, Brutus, Thrasea, Helvidius, and Dio; and gave me the idea of an equal commonwealth, with equal rights and equal speech, and also of a monarchy, where the liberty of the subject was principally regarded. To mention some more of my obligations to him:—It was of him I learned not to grow wise by starts and sudden fancies, but to be a constant admirer of philosophy and improvement; that a man ought to be generous and obliging, hope the best of matters, and never question the affection of his friends; to be free in showing a reasonable dislike of another, and no less clear in his own expectations and desires; and not to put his friends to the trouble of divining what he would be at.

15. I learned from Maximus to command myself, and not to be too much drawn towards anything; to be full of spirits under sickness and misfortune; to

appear with modesty, obligingness, and dignity of behaviour; to turn off business smoothly as it arises, without drudging and complaint. Whatever he did, all men believed him, that as he spoke, so he thought, and whatever he did, that he did with a good intent. He attained that greatness of mind, not to wonder or start at anything; neither to hurry an enterprise, nor sleep over it; never to be puzzled or dejected, nor to put on an appearance of friendliness; not to be angry or suspicious, but ever ready to do good, and to forgive and speak truth; and all this as one who seemed rather of himself to be straight and right, than ever to have been rectified. Nobody ever could fancy they were slighted by him, or dared to think themselves his betters. Besides all this, he had an agreeable wit.

16. In my adoptive father I observed a smooth and inoffensive temper, with great steadiness in keeping close to measures judiciously taken; a greatness proof against vanity and the impressions of pomp and power. From him a prince might learn to love business and action, and be constantly at it; to be willing to hear out any proposal relating to public advantage, and undeviatingly give every man his due; to understand the critical seasons and circumstances for rigour or remissness. To have no boy-favourites. Not to stand upon points of state and prerogative, but to leave his nobility at perfect liberty in their visits and attendance; and when he was upon his progress, no man lost his favour for not being at leisure to follow the court. To debate matters nicely

and thoroughly at the council-board, and then to stand by what was resolved on, yet not hastily to give up the inquiry, as one easily satisfied with sudden notions and apprehensions. To be constant to a friend, without tiring or fondness. To be always satisfied and cheerful. To reach forward into the future, and manage accordingly. Not to neglect the least concerns, but all without hurry, or being embarrassed. Farther, by observing his methods and administration, I had the opportunity of learning how much it was the part of a prince to check the excesses of panegyric and flattery. To have his magazines and exchequer well furnished. To be frugal in his expenses, without minding being lampooned for his pains. Not to worship the gods to superstition; not to court the populace, either by prodigality or compliment; but rather to be sober and firm upon all occasions, keeping things in a steady decorum, without chopping and changing of measures. To enjoy the plenty and magnificence of a sovereign fortune without bragging, and yet without making excuse; so as freely to enjoy them when present, but when wanting, not to be mortified at the loss of them. And to behave himself so that no man could charge him with sophistry, or buffooning, or being a pedant. No; he was a person mature and perfect, scorning flattery, and thoroughly qualified to govern himself and others. As for those that were philosophers in earnest, he had a great regard for them, but without reproaching those who were otherwise, nor yet being led away by these. He was condescending and familiar in conversation, and pleasant too, but not to tiresomeness and excess. As for his health, he was not anxious about it, like one fond of living, or over-studious of bodily appearance, and yet managed his constitution with that care as seldom to stand in need of the assistance of physic or outward applications. Farther, he never envied and browbeat those that were eminent in any faculty or science, as eloquence, or knowledge of the laws or morals; but, on the contrary, encouraged them in their ways, and promoted their reputation. He observed fitness and custom in all his actions, and yet did not seem to regard them. He was not fickle and fluttering in his humour, but constant both to place and undertaking; and I have seen him, after violent fits of the headache, return fresh and vigorous to his usual business. He kept but few things to himself, and those were secrets of government. He was very moderate and frugal in shows; public buildings, liberalities, and such like, being one that did not so much regard the popularity as the rightness of an action. It was none of his custom to bathe at unusual hours, or to be overcome with the fancy of building, to study eating and luxury, to value the curiosity of his clothes, or the shape and person of his servants. His cloak came from Lorium, his villa on the coast; at Lanuvium, he wore for the most part only a tunic; and at Tusculum he would scarcely so much as put on a cloak without making an excuse for it. To take him altogether, there was nothing of ruggedness, immodesty, or eagerness in his temper. Neither did he ever seem to drudge and sweat at the helm. Things were dispatched at leisure, and without being felt; and yet the administration was carried on without confusion, with great order, force, and uniformity. Upon the whole, what was told of Socrates is applicable to him; for he was so much master of himself, that he could either take or leave those conveniences of life with respect to which most people are either uneasy without them, or intemperate with them. Now, to hold on with fortitude in one condition and sobriety in the other is a proof of a great soul and an impregnable virtue, such as he showed in the sickness of Maximus.

17. I have to thank the gods that my grandfathers, parents, sister, preceptors, relations, friends, and domestics were almost all of them persons of probity, and that I never happened to disoblige or misbehave myself towards any of them, notwithstanding that my disposition was such, that, had occasion offered, I might have acted thus; but by the goodness of the gods, I met with no provocations to reveal my infirmities. It is likewise by their providence that my childhood was no longer managed by my grandfather's mistress; that I preserved the flower of my youth; that I was subject to the emperor my father, and bred under him, who was the most proper person living to put me out of conceit with pride, and to convince me that it is possible to live in a palace without the ceremony of guards, without richness and distinction of habit, without torches, statues, or such other marks of royalty and state; and that a prince may shrink himself almost into the figure of a private gentleman, and

yet act, nevertheless, with all the force and majesty of his character when the common weal requires it. It is the favour of the gods that I happened to meet with a brother, whose behaviour and affection is such as to contribute both to my pleasure and improvement. It is also their blessing that my children were neither stupid nor misshapen; that I made no farther advances in rhetoric, poetry, and such other amusements, which possibly might have engaged my fancy too far, had I found myself a considerable proficient; that, without asking, I gave my governors that share of honour which they seemed to desire, and did not put them off from time to time with promises and excuses, because they were yet but young; that I had the happiness of being acquainted with Apollonius, Rusticus, and Maximus; that I have a clear idea of the life in accordance with nature, and the impression frequently refreshed: so that, considering the extraordinary assistance and directions of the gods, it is impossible for me to miss the road of nature unless by refusing to be guided by the dictates and almost sensible inspirations of heaven. It is by their favour that my constitution has held out so well, under a life of fatigue and business; that I never had to do with Benedicta or Theodotus; and, when I fell into some fits of love, I was soon cured; that when I fell out with Rusticus, as it frequently happened, I was not transported into any act of violence; that I had the satisfaction of my mother's life and company a considerable while, though she was destined to die young; that when I was willing to relieve the necessities of others, I was never told that the exchequer was empty; and, again, it is they that kept me from standing in need of any man's fortune. Farther, it is from them that my wife is so very obedient and affectionate, and so remote from luxury; that I had choice of good governors for my children; that remedies were prescribed me in a dream against giddiness and spitting of blood, as at Cajeta, by an ointment; that when I had a mind to look into philosophy, I did not meet with a sophist to instruct me; that I did not spend too much time in reading history, chopping logic, or considering the heavens. Now all these points could never have been compassed without a protection from above and the gods presiding over fate.

This was written in the country of the Quadi, at the Granua.

BOOK II.

BOOK II.

1. REMEMBER to put yourself in mind every morning, that before night it will be your luck to meet with some busy-body, with some ungrateful, abusive fellow, with some knavish, envious, or unsociable churl or other. Now all this perverseness in them proceeds from their ignorance of good and evil; and since it has fallen to my share to understand the natural beauty of a good action, and the deformity of an ill one—since I am satisfied the person disobliging is of kin to me, and though we are not just of the same flesh and blood, yet our minds are nearly related, being both extracted from the Deity—I am likewise convinced that no man can do me a real injury, because no man can force me to misbehave myself, nor can I find it in my heart to hate or to be angry with one of my own nature and family. For we are all made for mutual assistance, as the feet, the hands, and the eyelids, as the rows of the upper and under teeth, from whence it follows that clashing and opposition is perfectly unnatural. Now such an unfriendly disposition is implied in resentment and aversion.

2. This being of mine, all there is of it, consists of flesh, breath, and the ruling part. Away with your books then. Suffer not your mind any more to be distracted. It is not permitted. As for your body, value it no more than if you were just expiring. For what is it? Nothing but a little blood and bones; a piece of network, wrought out of nerves, veins, and arteries twisted together. In the next place, consider what sort of thing your breath is; why, only a little air, and that not constant, but every moment let out of your lungs, and sucked in again. The third part of your composition is the ruling part. Now consider thus: you are an old man: do not suffer this noble part of you under servitude any longer. Let it not be moved by the springs of selfish passions; let it not quarrel with fate, be uneasy at the present, or afraid of the future.

3. Providence shines clearly through the works of the gods; even the works of chance are not without dependence on Nature, being only an effect of that chain of causes which are under a providential regulation. Indeed, all things flow from this fountain; besides, there is necessity, and the interest of the whole universe, of which you are a part. Now, that which is both the product and support of universal Nature, must by consequence be serviceable to every part of it; but the world subsists upon change, and is preserved by the mutation of the simple elements, and also of things mixed and compounded, and what it loses one way it gets another. Let these reflections satisfy you, and make them your rule to live by. As

for books, cast away your thirst after them, that you may not die complaining, but go off in good-humour, and heartily thank the gods for what you have had.

4. Remember how often you have postponed minding your interest, and let slip those opportunities the gods have given you. It is now high time to consider what sort of world you are part of, and from what kind of governor of it you are descended; that you have a set period assigned you to act in, and unless you improve it to brighten and compose your thoughts, it will quickly run off with you, and be lost beyond recovery.

5. Take care always to remember that you are a man and a Roman; and let every action be done with perfect and unaffected gravity, humanity, freedom, and justice. And be sure you entertain no fancies, which may give check to these qualities. This is possible, if you will but perform every action as though it were your last; if your appetites and passions do not cross upon your reason; if you keep clear of rashness, and have nothing of insincerity and self-love to infect you, and do not complain of your destiny. You see what a few points a man has to gain in order to attain to a godlike way of living; for he that comes thus far, performs all which the immortal powers will require of him.

6. Continue to dishonour yourself, my soul! Neither will you have much time left to do yourself honour. For the life of each man is almost up already; and yet, instead of paying a due regard to yourself, you place your happiness in the souls of other men.

7. Do not let accidents disturb, or outward objects engross your thoughts, but keep your mind quiet and disengaged, that you may be at leisure to learn something good, and cease rambling from one thing to another. There is likewise another sort of roving to be avoided; for some people are busy and yet do nothing; they fatigue and wear themselves out, and yet aim at no goal, nor propose any general end of action or design.

8. A man can rarely be unhappy by being ignorant of another's thoughts; but he that does not attend to the motions of his own is certainly unhappy.

9. These reflections ought always to be at hand:—To consider well the nature of the universe and my own nature, together with the relation betwixt them, and what kind of part it is, of what kind of whole; and that no mortal can hinder me from acting and speaking conformably to the being of which I am a part.

10. Theophrastus, in comparing the degrees of faults (as men would commonly distinguish them), talks like a philosopher when he affirms that those instances of misbehaviour which proceed from desire are greater than those of which anger is the occasion. For a man that is angry seems to quit his hold of reason unwillingly and with pain, and start out of rule before he is aware. But he that runs riot out of desire, being overcome by pleasure, loses all hold on himself, and all manly restraint. Well, then, and like a philosopher, he said that he of the two is the more to be condemned that sins with pleasure than he that sins with grief. For the first looks like an injured

person, and is vexed, and, as it were, forced into a passion; whereas the other begins with inclination, and commits the fault through desire.

11. Manage all your actions, words, and thoughts accordingly, since you may at any moment quit life. And what great matter is the business of dying? If the gods are in being, you can suffer nothing, for they will do you no harm. And if they are not, or take no care of us mortals—why, then, a world without either gods or Providence is not worth a man's while to live in. But, in truth, the being of the gods, and their concern in human affairs, is beyond dispute. And they have put it entirely in a man's power not to fall into any calamity properly so-called. And if other misfortunes had been really evils, they would have provided against them too, and furnished man with capacity to avoid them. But how can that which cannot make the man worse make his life so? I can never be persuaded that the universal Nature neglected these matters through want of knowledge, or, having that, yet lacked the power to prevent or correct the error; or that Nature should commit such a fault, through want of power or skill, as to suffer things, really good and evil, to happen promiscuously to good and bad men. Now, living and dying, honour and infamy, pleasure and pain, riches and poverty—all these things are the common allotment of the virtuous and vicious, because they have nothing intrinsically noble or base in their nature; and, therefore, to speak properly, are neither good nor bad.

12. Consider how quickly all things are dissolved and resolved; the bodies and substances themselves into the matter and substance of the world, and their memories into its general age and time. Consider, too, the objects of sense, particularly those which charm us with pleasure, frighten us with pain, or are most admired for empty reputation. The power of thought will show a man how insignificant, despicable, and paltry these things are, and how soon they wither and die. It will show him what those people are upon whose fancy and good word the being of fame depends: also the nature of death, which, if once abstracted from the pomp and terror of the idea, will be found nothing more than a pure natural action. Now he that dreads the course of nature is a very child; but this is not only a work of nature, but is also profitable to her. Lastly, we should consider how we are related to the Deity, and in what part of our being, and in what condition of that part.

13. Nothing can be more unhappy than the curiosity of that man that ranges everywhere, and digs into the earth, as the poet says, for discovery; that is wonderfully busy to force by conjecture a passage into other people's thoughts, but does not consider that it is sufficient to reverence and serve the divinity within himself. And this service consists in this, that a man keep himself pure from all violent passion, and evil affection, from all rashness and vanity, and from all manner of discontent towards gods or men. For as for the gods, their administration ought to be revered upon the score of excellency;

and as for men, their actions should be well taken for the sake of common kindred. Besides, they are often to be pitied for their ignorance of good and evil; which incapacity of discerning between moral qualities is no less a defect than that of a blind man, who cannot distinguish between white and black.

14. Though you were to live three thousand, or, if you please, thirty thousand of years, yet remember that no man can lose any other life than that which he now lives, neither is he possessed of any other than that which he loses. Whence it follows that the longest life, as we commonly speak, and the shortest, come all to the same reckoning. For the present is of the same duration everywhere. Everybody's loss, therefore, is of the same bigness, and reaches no further than to a point of time, for no man is capable of losing either the past or the future; for how can one be deprived of what he has not? So that under this consideration there are two notions worth remembering. One is, that Nature treads in a circle, and has much the same face through the whole course of eternity. And therefore it signifies not at all whether a man stands gazing here an hundred, or two hundred, or an infinity of years; for all that he gets by it is only to see the same sights so much the oftener. The other hint is, that when the longest and shortest-lived persons come to die, their loss is equal; they can but lose the present as being the only thing they have; for that which he has not, no man can be truly said to lose.

15. Monimus, the Cynic philosopher, used to say

that all things were but opinion. Now this saying may undoubtedly prove serviceable, provided one accepts it only as far as it is true.

16. There are several different ways by which a man's soul may do violence to itself; first of all, when it becomes an abscess, and, as it were, an excrescence on the universe, as far as in it lies. For to be vexed at anything that happens is a separation of ourselves from nature, in some part of which the natures of all other things are contained. Secondly, it falls under the same misfortune when it hates any person, or goes against him, with an intention of mischief, which is the case of the angry and revengeful. Thirdly, it wrongs itself when it is overcome by pleasure or pain. Fourthly, when it makes use of art, tricking, and falsehood, in word or action. Fifthly, when it does not know what it would be at in a business, but runs on without thought or design, whereas even the least undertaking ought to be aimed at some end. Now the end of rational beings is to be governed by the law and reason of the most venerable city and constitution.

17. The extent of human life is but a point; its substance is in perpetual flux, its perceptions dim, and the whole composition of the body tending to corruption. The soul is but a whirl, fortune not to be guessed at, and fame undiscerning—in a word, that which belongs to the body is a flowing river, and what the soul has is but dream and bubble. Life is but a campaign, or course of travels, and after-fame is oblivion. What is it, then, that will stick by a man?

Why, nothing but philosophy. Now, this consists in keeping the divinity within us from injury and disgrace, superior to pleasure and pain, doing nothing at random, without any dissembling and pretence, and independent of the motions of another. Farther, philosophy brings the mind to take things as they fall, and acquiesce in their distribution, inasmuch as all events proceed from the same cause with itself; and, above all, to have an easy prospect of death, as being nothing more than a dissolving of the elements of which each thing is composed. Now, if the elements themselves are never the worse for running off one into another, what if they should all change and be dissolved? Why should any man be concerned at the consequence? All this is but Nature's method; now, Nature never does any mischief.

Written at Carnuntum.

BOOK III.

BOOK III.

1. WE ought not only to remember that life is wearing off, and a smaller part of it is left daily, but also to consider that if a man's life should happen to be longer than ordinary, yet it is uncertain whether his mind will keep pace with his years, and afford him sense enough for business, and power to contemplate things human and divine. For if the man begins to dote, it is true the mere animal life goes on; he may breathe, and be nourished, and be furnished with imagination and appetite; but to make any proper use of himself, to fill up the measure of his duty, to distinguish appearances, and to know whether it is time for him to walk out of the world or not—as to all such noble functions of reason and judgment, the man is perfectly dead already. It concerns us, therefore, to push forward, and make the most of our matters, for death is continually advancing; and besides that, our understanding sometimes dies before us.

2. It is worth while to observe that the least thing that happens naturally to things natural has something in itself that is pleasing and delightful.

Thus, for example, there are cracks and little breaks on the surface of a loaf, which, though never intended by the baker, have a sort of agreeableness in them, which invites the appetite. Thus figs, when they are most ripe, open and gape; and olives, when they fall of themselves and are near decaying, are particularly pretty to look at. The bending of an ear of corn, the brow of a lion, the foam of a boar, and many other things, if you take them singly, are far enough from being beautiful; but when they are looked on as effects of the products of Nature, help to adorn and attract. Thus, if a man has but inclination and thought enough to examine the product of the universe, he will find the most unpromising appearances in the results of Nature not without charm, and that the more remote appendages have somewhat to recommend them. One thus prepared will be no less pleased to see the gaping jaws of living beasts than the imitations of painters and sculptors, and with chastened eyes he will find beauty in the ripeness of age as well as in the blossom of youth. I grant many of these things will not charm everyone, but only those who are truly in harmony with Nature and her works.

3. Hippocrates, who cured so many diseases, himself fell ill and died. The Chaldeans, who foretold other people's death, at last met with their own fate. Alexander, Pompey, and Julius Cæsar, who had destroyed so many towns, and cut off so many thousands of horse and foot in the field, were forced at last to march off themselves. Heraclitus, who argued so much about the universal conflagration, died

through water by a dropsy. Democritus was eaten up with vermin; another sort of vermin destroyed Socrates. What are these instances for? Look you: you have embarked, you have made your voyage and your port; debark then without more ado. If you happen to land upon another world, there will be gods enough to take care of you; but if it be your fortune to drop into nothing, why, then you will be no more solicited with pleasure and pain. Then you will have done drudging for your outer covering, which is the more unworthy in proportion as that which serves it is worthy; for the one is all soul, intelligence, and divinity, whereas the other is but dirt and corruption.

4. For the future, do not spend your thoughts upon other people, unless you are led to it by common interest. For the prying into foreign business—that is, musing upon the talk, fancies, and contrivances of another, and guessing at the what and why of his actions—does but make a man forget himself, and ramble from his own guiding principle. He ought, therefore, not to work his mind to no purpose, nor throw a superfluous link into the chain of thought; and more especially, to avoid curiosity and malice in his inquiry. Accustom yourself, therefore, to think upon nothing but what you could freely reveal, if the question were put to you; so that if your soul were thus laid open, there would nothing appear but what was sincere, good-natured, and public-spirited—not so much as one voluptuous or luxurious fancy, nothing of hatred, envy, or unreasonable suspicion, nor aught else which you could not bring to the light without

blushing. A man thus qualified, who does not delay to assume the first rank among mortals, is a sort of priest and minister of the gods, and makes a right use of the Deity within him. By the assistance thereof, he is preserved, uninfected with pleasure, invulnerable against pain—out of the reach of injury, and above the malice of evil people. Thus he wrestles in the noblest fight, to hold his own against all his passions; and penetrated with the spirit of justice, welcomes with his whole heart all that happens and is allotted to him. He never minds other people's speech, thoughts, or actions, unless public necessity and general good require it. No; he keeps himself to his own business, and contemplates that portion of the whole allotted him by the fates, and endeavours to do the first as it should be, and believes that his lot is good. For every man's fate is suitable, since it is suited to him. He considers that the rational principle is akin in all men, and that general kindness and concern for the whole world is no more than a piece of human nature—that not every one's good opinion is not worth the gaining, but only that of those who seek to live in accordance with Nature. As for others, he knows their way of living, both at home and abroad, by day and by night, and their companions in their evil way of life, and he bears it in mind. And, why, indeed, should he value the commendation of such people, who are not able even to please themselves?

5. Be not unwilling, selfish, unadvised, or passionate in anything you do. Do not affect quaintness and points of wit: neither talk nor meddle more

than is necessary. Take care that the divinity within you has a creditable charge to preside over; that you appear in the character of your sex and age. Act like a Roman Emperor that loves his country, and be always in a readiness to quit the field at the first summons; and ere you claim your discharge, manage your credit so, that you need neither swear yourself nor want a voucher. Let your air be cheerful; depend not upon external supports, nor beg your tranquillity of another. And, in a word, never throw away your legs, to stand upon crutches.

6. If, in the whole compass of human life, you find anything preferable to justice and truth; to temperance and fortitude; to a mind self-satisfied with its own rational conduct, and entirely resigned to fate—if, I say, you know anything better than this, turn to it with your whole soul, and enjoy it, accounting it the best. But if there is nothing more valuable than the divinity implanted within you, and this is master of its appetites, examines all impressions, and has detached itself from the senses, as Socrates used to say, and shows itself submissive to the government of the gods, and helpful and benevolent to mankind—if all things are trifles compared with this, give way to nothing else. For if you are once inclined to any such thing, it will no longer be in your power to give your undivided preference to what is your own peculiar good, for it is not lawful that anything of another kind or nature, as either popular applause, or power, or riches, or pleasures, should be suffered to contest with what is rationally and politically good.

All these things, if but for a while they begin to please, presently prevail, and pervert a man's mind. Let your choice therefore run all one way, and be bold and resolute for that which is best. Now what is profitable is best. If that means profitable to man as he is a rational being, stand to it; but if it means profitable to him as a mere animal, reject it, and keep your judgment without arrogance. Only take care to make inquiry secure.

7. Think nothing for your interest which makes you break your word, quit your modesty, hate, suspect, or curse any person, or inclines you to any practice which will not bear the light and look the world in the face. For he that values his mind and the worship of his divinity before all other things, need act no tragic part, laments under no misfortune, and wants neither solitude nor company; and, which is still more, he will neither fly from life nor pursue it, but is perfectly indifferent about the length or shortness of the time in which his soul shall be encompassed by his body. And if he were to expire this moment, he is as ready for it as for any other action that may be performed with modesty and decency. For all his life long, this is his only care—that his mind may always be occupied as befits a rational and social creature.

8. If you examine a man that has been well-disciplined and purified by philosophy, you will find nothing that is unsound, foul, or false in him. Death can never surprise his life as imperfect, so that nobody can say he goes off the stage before his part is

quite played. Besides, there is in him nothing servile or affected; he neither attaches himself too closely to others, nor keeps aloof from them; he is neither responsible to them, nor does he avoid them.

9. Hold in honour your opinionative faculty, for this alone is able to prevent any opinion from originating in your guiding principle that is contrary to Nature or the proper constitution of a rational creature. Now, a rational constitution enjoins us to do nothing rashly, and to be kindly disposed towards men, and to submit willingly to the gods.

10. As for other speculations, throw them all out of your head, excepting those few precepts above mentioned—remembering withal, that every man's life lies all within the present, which is but a point of time; for the past is spent, and the future is uncertain. Life moves in a very narrow compass; yes, and men live in a small corner of the world too. And the most lasting fame will stretch but to a sorry extent; for, alas! poor transitory mortals who hand it down know little even of themselves, much less of those who died long before their time.

11. To the foregoing hints you may add this which follows:—make for yourself a particular description and definition of every object that presents itself to your mind, that you may thoroughly contemplate it in its own nature, bare and naked, wholly and separately. And in your own mind call itself and the parts of which it is composed, and into which it will be resolved, by its own and proper name; for nothing is so likely to raise the mind

to a pitch of greatness as the power truly and methodically to examine and consider all things that happen in this life, and so to penetrate into their natures as to apprehend at once what sort of purpose each thing serves, and what sort of universe makes use of it—what value it bears to the whole, and what to man, who is a citizen of that great capital, in respect of which all other towns are no more than single families—what is this object which makes an impression on me; how long can it last; what virtue does it require of me; is it good-nature, fortitude, truth, simplicity, self-sufficiency, or any of the rest? On each occasion a man should be ready to pronounce, "This was sent me by heaven, this by destiny, or the combinations of fate, or by one of the same clan, or family, or company as myself, who knows not what is natural for him. But I do know; therefore I am just and friendly to him, and treat him according to the natural laws of our communion. However, in things indifferent I take care to rate them according to their respective value."

12. If you will be governed by reason, and manage what lies before you with industry, vigour, and temper; if you will not run out after new distraction, but keep your divinity pure, even as though you must at once render it up again, your mind staunch and well disciplined, as if this trial of behaviour were your last; and, if you will but cleave to this, and be true to the best of yourself, fearing and desiring nothing, but living up to your nature, standing boldly by the truth of your word, and satisfied therewith,

then you will be a happy man. But the whole world cannot hinder you from so doing.

13. As surgeons always have their instruments and knives ready for sudden occasions, so be you always furnished with rules and principles to let you into the knowledge of things human and divine, remembering even in your slightest action the connection these two have with each other. For without a regard for things divine, you will fail in your behaviour towards men; and again, the reasoning holds for the other side of the argument.

14. Wander at random no longer. Alas! you have no time left to peruse your diary, to read over the Greek and Roman history, or so much as your own commonplace book, which you collected to serve you when you were old. Hasten then towards the goal. Do not flatter and deceive yourself. Come to your own aid while yet you may, if you have a kindness for yourself.

15. Men do not know in how many senses they can take the words *to steal, to buy, to sow, to be quiet, to see what should be done;* for this is not effected by eyes, but by another kind of vision.

16. There are three things which belong to a man—body, soul, and mind. Sensation belongs to the body, impulse to the soul, and reason to the mind. To have the senses stamped with the impression of an object is common to brutes and cattle; to be hurried and convulsed with passion is the quality of beasts of prey and men of pleasure—such as Phalaris and Nero—of atheists and traitors, too, and of those who do

not care what they do when no man sees them. Now, since these qualities are common, let us find out the mark of a man of probity. His distinction, then, lies in letting reason guide his practice, in contentment with all that is allotted him, keeping pure the divinity within him, untroubled by a crowd of appearances, preserving it tranquil, and obeying it as a god. He is all truth in his words and justice in his actions; and if the whole world should disbelieve his integrity, dispute his character, and question his happiness, he would neither take it ill in the least, nor turn aside from that path that leads to the aim of life, towards which he must move pure, calm, well-prepared, and with perfect resignation in his fate.

BOOK IV.

BOOK IV.

1. WHEN the mind acts up to Nature, she is rightly disposed, and takes things as they come, and tacks about with her circumstances; as for fixing the condition of her activity, she is not at all solicitous about that. It is true, she is not perfectly indifferent; she moves forward with a preference in her choice; but if anything comes cross, she falls to work upon it, and like fire converts it into fuel; for like this element, when it is weak, it is easily put out, but when once well kindled it seizes upon what is heaped upon it, subdues it into its own nature, and increases by resistance.

2. Let every action tend to some point, and be perfect in its kind.

3. It is the custom of people to go to unfrequented places and country places and the sea-shore and the mountains for retirement; and this you often earnestly desired. But, after all, this is but a vulgar fancy, for it is in your power to withdraw into yourself whenever you desire. Now one's own mind is a place the most free from crowd and noise in the world, if a man's thoughts are such as to ensure him perfect

tranquillity within, and this tranquillity consists in the good ordering of the mind. Your way is, therefore, to make frequent use of this retirement, and refresh your virtue in it. And to this end, be always provided with a few short, uncontested notions, to keep your understanding true, and send you back content with the business to which you return. For instance: What is it that troubles you? It is the wickedness of the world. If this be your case, out with your antidote, and consider that rational beings were made for mutual advantage, that forbearance is one part of justice, and that people misbehave themselves against their will. Consider, likewise, how many men have embroiled themselves, and spent their days in disputes, suspicion, and animosities; and now they are dead, and burnt to ashes. Be quiet, then, and disturb yourself no more. But, it may be, the distribution of the world does not please you. Recall the alternative, and argue thus: either Providence or atoms rule the universe. Besides, you may recall the proofs that the world is, as it were, one great city and corporation. But possibly the ill state of your health afflicts you. Pray reflect, your intellect is not affected by the roughness or smoothness of the currents of sensation, if she will retire and take a view of her own privilege and power. And when she has done this, recollect the philosophy about pleasure and pain, to which you have even now listened and assented. Well! it may be the concern of fame sits hard upon you. If you are pinched here, consider how quickly all things vanish, and are forgotten—what an immense chaos there stands on either side of eternity. Applause! consider the emptiness of the sound, the precarious tenure, the little judgment of those that give it us, and the narrow compass it is confined to; for the whole globe is but a point; and of this little, how small is your habitation, and how insignificant the number and quality of your admirers. Upon the whole, do not forget to retire into the little realm of your own. And, above all things, let there be no straining nor struggling in the case, but move freely, and contemplate matters like a human being, a citizen, and a mortal. And among the rest of your stock, let these two maxims be always ready: first, that things cannot disturb the soul, but remain motionless without, while disturbance springs from the opinion within the soul. The second is, to consider that the scene is just shifting and sliding off into nothing; and that you yourself have seen abundance of great alterations. In a word, the world is all transformation, and life is opinion.

4. If the faculty of understanding lies in common amongst us all, then reason, the cause of it, must be common too; and that other reason too which governs practice by commands and prohibitions. From whence we may conclude, that mankind are under one common law; and if so, they must be fellow-citizens, and belong to some body politic. From whence it will follow, that the whole world is but one commonwealth; for certainly there is no other society in which mankind can be incorporated. Now this common fund of understanding, reason, and law is a

commodity of this same country, or which way do mortals light on it? For as the four distinctions in my body belong to some general head and species of matter; for instance, the earthy part in me comes from the division of earth; the watery belongs to another element; the airy particles flow from a third spring, and those of fire from one distinct from all the former (for nothing can no more produce something, than something can sink into nothing); thus it is evident that our understanding must proceed from some source or other.

5. Death and generation are both mysteries of nature, and somewhat resemble each other; for the first does but dissolve those elements the latter had combined. Now there is nothing that a man need be ashamed of in all this; nothing that is opposed to his nature as a rational being, and to the design of his constitution.

6. Practices and dispositions are generally of a piece; such usage from such sort of men is in a manner necessary. To be surprised at it, is in effect to wonder that the fig-tree yields juice. Pray consider that both you and your enemy are dropping off, and that ere long your very memories will be extinguished.

7. Do not suppose you are hurt, and your complaint ceases. Cease your complaint, and you are not hurt.

8. That which does not make a man worse, does not make his life worse; and by consequence he has no harm either within or without.

9. The nature of the general good was obliged to act in this manner.

10. Take notice that all events turn out justly, and that if you observe nicely, you will not only perceive a connection between causes and effects, but a sovereign distribution of justice, which presides in the administration, and gives everything its due. Observe, then, as you have begun, and let all your actions answer the character of a good man—I mean a good man in the strictness and notion of philosophy.

11. If a man affronts you, do not accept his opinion or think just as he would have you do. No, look upon things as reality presents them.

12. Be always provided with principles for these two purposes :—*First,* To engage in nothing but what reason dictates, what the sovereign and legislative part of you shall suggest, for the interest of mankind. *Secondly,* To be disposed to quit your opinion, and alter your measures, when a friend shall give you good grounds for so doing. But then the reasons of changing your mind ought to be drawn from some consideration regarding justice and public good, or some such generous motive, and not because it pleases your fancy, or promotes your reputation.

13. Have you any sense in your head? Yes. Why do you not make use of it then? For if this faculty does but do its part, I cannot see what more you need wish for.

14. At present your nature is distinct; but ere long you will vanish into the whole. Or, rather, you will be returned into that universal reason which gave you your being.

15. When frankincense is thrown upon the altar, one grain usually falls before another; but it makes no difference.

16. Do but return to the principles of wisdom, and those who take you now for a monkey or a wild beast, will make a god of you in a week's time.

17. Do not act as if you had ten thousand years to throw away. Death stands at your elbow. Be good for something, while you live and it is in your power.

18. What a great deal of time and ease that man gains who lets his neighbour's words, thoughts, and behaviour alone, confines his inspections to himself, and takes care that his own actions are honest and righteous. "Truly," as Agathon observes, "we should not wander thus, but run straight to the goal without rambling and impertinence."

19. He that is so very solicitous about being talked of when he is dead, and makes his memory his inclination, does not consider that all who knew him will quickly be gone. That his fame will grow less in the next generation, and flag upon the course; and handed from one to another by men who eagerly desire it themselves, and are quenched themselves, it will be quenched at last; but granting your memory and your men immortal, what is their panegyric to you? I do not say, when you are dead, but if you were living, what would commendation signify, unless for some reason of utility? To conclude; if you depend thus servilely upon the good word of other people, you will be unworthy of your nature.

20. Whatever is good has that quality from itself; it is finished by its own nature, and commendation is no part of it. Why, then, a thing is neither better nor worse for being praised. This holds concerning things which are called good in the common way of speaking, as the products of nature and art; what do you think, then, of that which deserves this character in the strictest propriety? It wants nothing foreign to complete the idea any more than law, truth, good nature, and sobriety. Do any of these virtues stand in need of a good word, or are they the worse for a bad one? I hope an emerald will shine nevertheless for a man's being silent about the worth of it. Neither is there any necessity of praising gold, ivory, purple, a lyre, a dagger, a little flower, or a shrub.

21. If human souls have a being after death, which way has the air made room for them from all eternity? Pray, how has the earth been capacious enough to receive all the bodies buried in it? The resolution of this latter question will satisfy the former. For as a corpse after some continuance by change and dissolution makes way for another, so when a man dies, and the spirit is let loose into the air, it holds out for some time, after which it is changed, diffused, and kindled in flame, or else absorbed into the generative principle of the universe. And thus they make room for succession. And this may serve for an answer upon the supposition of the soul's surviving the body. Besides, we are not only to consider the vast number of bodies disposed of in the manner above mentioned; but what an infinite number are every day devoured

by mankind, and other living creatures, and as it were buried in their bodies. And yet by the transmutation of the food into blood, or into fire and air, there is space enough. And now which way can a man investigate the truth? Why, in order to this, he must divide the thing in question into the causal and material elements.

22. Do not run riot; keep your intentions honest, and your convictions sure.

23. Whatever is agreeable to you, O Universe, is so to me too. Nothing is early or late for me that is seasonable for you. Everything is fruit for me which your seasons bring, oh Nature. From you all things proceed, subsist in you, and return to you. And if the poet said, "Dear City of Cecrops," may we not also say, "Dear City of God"?

24. "If you would live at your ease," says Democritus, "manage but a few things." I think it had been better if he had said, "Do nothing but what is necessary; and what becomes the reason of a social being, and in the order too it prescribes it." For by this rule a man has the double pleasure of making his actions good and few into the bargain. For the greater part of what we say and do, being unnecessary, if this were but once retrenched, we should have both more leisure and less disturbance. And therefore before a man sets forward he should ask himself this question, "Am I not upon the verge of something unnecessary?" Farther, we should apply this hint to what we think, as well as to what we do. For impertinence of thought draws unnecessary action after it.

25. Make an experiment upon yourself, and examine your proficiency in a life of virtue. Try how you can acquiesce in your fate, and whether your own honesty and good nature will content you.

26. Have you seen this side? Pray view the other too. Never be disturbed, but let your purpose be single. Is any man guilty of a fault? It is to himself then. Has any advantage happened to you? It is the bounty of fate. It was all of it preordained you by the universal cause, and woven in your destiny from the beginning. On the whole, life is but short, therefore be just and prudent, and make the most of it. And when you divert yourself, be always upon your guard.

27. The world is either the effect of contrivance or chance; if the latter, it is a world for all that, that is to say, it is a regular and beautiful structure. Now can any man discover symmetry in his own shape, and yet take the universe for a heap of disorder? I say the universe, in which the very discord and confusion of the elements settles into harmony and order.

28. A black character, an effeminate character, an obstinate character, brutish, savage, childish, silly, false, scurrilous, mercenary, tyrannical.

29. Not to know what is in the world, and not to know what is done in the world, comes much to the same thing, and a man is one way no less a stranger than the other. He is no better than a deserter that flies from public law. He is a blind man that shuts the eyes of his understanding; and he is a beggar that is not furnished at home, but wants the assistance

of another. He that frets himself because things do not happen just as he would have them, and secedes and separates himself from the law of universal nature, is but a sort of an ulcer of the world, never considering that the same cause which produced the displeasing accident made him too. And lastly, he that is selfish, and cuts off his own soul from the universal soul of all rational beings, is a kind of voluntary outlaw.

30. This philosopher has never a tunic to his coat, the other never a book to read, and a third is half naked, and yet they are none of them discouraged. One learned man says, "I have no bread, yet I abide by reason." Another, "I have no profit of my learning, yet I too abide by reason."

31. Be satisfied with your business, and learn to love what you were bred to; and as to the remainder of your life, be entirely resigned, and let the gods do their pleasure with your body and your soul. And when this is done, be neither slave nor tyrant to anybody.

32. To begin somewhere, consider how the world went in Vespasian's time; consider this, I say, and you will find mankind just at the same pass they are now: some marrying and some concerned in education, some sick and some dying, some fighting and some feasting, some drudging at the plough and some upon the exchange; some too affable and some overgrown with conceit; one full of jealousy and the other of knavery. Here you might find a group wishing for the death of their friends, and there a

seditious club complaining of the times. Some were lovers and some misers, some grasped at the consulship and some at the sceptre. Well! all is over with that generation long since. Come forward then to the reign of Trajan. Now here you will find the same thing, but they are all gone too. Go on with the contemplation, and carry it to other times and countries, and here you will see abundance of people very busy with their projects, who are quickly resolved into their elements. More particularly recollect those within your own memory, who have been hurried on in these vain pursuits; how they have overlooked the dignity of their nature, and neglected to hold fast to that, and be satisfied with it. And here you must remember to proportion your concern to the weight and importance of each action. Thus, if you refrain from trifling, you may part with amusements without regret.

33. Those words which were formerly current are now become obsolete. Alas! this is not all; fame tarnishes in time too, and men grow out of fashion as well as language. Those celebrated names of Camillus, Cæso, Volesus, and Leonnatus are antiquated. Those of Scipio, Cato, and Augustus will soon have the same fortune, and those of Hadrian and Antoninus must follow. All these things are transitory, and quickly become as a tale that is told, and are swallowed up in oblivion. I speak this of those who have been the wonder of their age and who shone with unusual lustre. But as for the rest, they are no sooner dead than forgotten. And after all, what does fame everlasting

mean? Mere vanity. What then is it that is worth one's while to be concerned for? Why nothing but this: to bear an honest mind, to act for the good of society, to deceive nobody, to welcome everything that happens as necessary and familiar, and flowing from a like source.

34. Put yourself frankly into the hands of fate, and let her spin you out what fortune she pleases.

35. He that does a memorable action, and those that report it, are all but short-lived things.

36. Accustom yourself to consider that whatever is produced, is produced by alteration; that nature loves nothing so much as changing existing things, and producing new ones like them. For that which exists at present is, as it were, the seed of what shall spring from it. But if you take seed in the common notion, and confine it to the field or the womb, you have a dull fancy.

37. You are just taking leave of the world, and yet you have not done with unnecessary desires. Are you not yet above disturbance and suspicion, and fully convinced that nothing without can hurt you? You have not yet learned to be friends with everybody, and that to be an honest man is the only way to be a wise one.

38. To understand the true quality of people, you must look into their minds, and examine their pursuits and aversions.

39. Your pain cannot originate in another man's mind, nor in any change or transformation of your corporeal covering. Where then does it lie? Why,

in that part of you that forms judgments about things evil. Do not imagine you are hurt, and you are impregnable. Suppose then your flesh was hacked, burnt, putrified, or mortified, yet let that part that judges keep quiet; that is, do not conclude that what is common to good or ill men can be good or evil in itself. For that which may be everybody's lot, must in its own nature be indifferent.

40. You ought frequently to consider that the world is an animal, consisting of one soul and body, that an universal sense runs through the whole mass of matter. You should likewise reflect how nature acts by a joint effort, and how everything contributes to the being of everything: and lastly, what connection and subordination there is between causes and effects.

41. Epictetus will tell you that you are a living soul, that drags a corpse about with her.

42. Things that subsist upon change, and owe their being to instability, can neither be considerably good nor bad.

43. Time is like a rapid river, and a rushing torrent of all that comes and passes. A thing is no sooner well come, but it is past; and then another is borne after it, and this too will be carried away.

44. Whatever happens is as common and well known as a rose in the spring, or an apple in autumn. Of this kind are diseases and death, calumny and trickery, and every other thing which raises and depresses the spirits of unthinking people.

45. Antecedents and consequents are dexterously

tied together in the world. Things are not carelessly thrown on a heap, and joined more by number than nature, but, as it were, rationally connected with each other. And as the things that exist are harmoniously connected, so those that become exhibit no mere succession, but an harmonious relationship.

46. Do not forget the saying of Heraclitus, "That the earth dies into water, water into air, air into fire, and so backward." Remember likewise the story of the man that travelled on without knowing to what place the way would bring him; and that many people quarrel with that reason that governs the world, and with which they are daily conversant, and seem perfectly unacquainted with those things which occur daily. Farther, we must not nod over business—for even in sleep we seem to act,—neither are we to be wholly governed by tradition; for that is like children, who believe anything their parents tell them.

47. Put the case, some god should acquaint you you were to die to-morrow, or next day at farthest. Under this warning, you would be a very poor wretch if you should strongly solicit for the longest time. For, alas! how inconsiderable is the difference? In like manner, if you would reason right, you would not be much concerned whether your life was to end to-morrow or a thousand years hence.

48. Consider how many physicians are dead that used to knit their brows over their patients; how many astrologers who thought themselves great men by foretelling the death of others; how many philosophers have gone the way of all flesh, after all their

learned disputes about dying and immortality; how many warriors, who had knocked so many men's brains out; how many tyrants, who managed the power of life and death with as much insolence, as if themselves had been immortal; how many cities, if I may say so, have given up the ghost: for instance, Helice in Greece, Pompeii and Herculaneum in Italy; not to mention many besides. Do but recollect your acquaintance, and here you will find one man closing another's eyes, then he himself is laid out, and this one by another. And all within a small compass of time. In short, mankind are poor transitory things! They are one day in the rudiments of life, and almost the next turned to mummy or ashes. Your way is therefore to manage this minute in harmony with nature, and part with it cheerfully; and like a ripe olive when you drop, be sure to speak well of the mother that bare you, and make your acknowledgments to the tree that produced you.

49. Stand firm like a rock, against which though the waves batter, yet it stands unmoved, and they fall to rest at last. How unfortunate has this accident made me, cries such an one! Not at all! He should rather say, What a happy mortal am I for being unconcerned upon this occasion! for being neither crushed by the present, nor afraid of what is to come. The thing might have happened to any other man as well as myself; but for all that, everybody would not have been so easy under it. Why then is not the good fortune of the bearing more considerable than the ill fortune of the happening? Or, to speak

properly, how can that be a misfortune to a man which does not frustrate his nature? And how can that cross upon a man's nature which is not opposed to the intention and design of it? Now what that intention is, you know. To apply this reasoning: does the present accident hinder your being just, magnanimous, temperate and modest, judicious, truthful, reverent, and unservile? Now, when a man is furnished with these good qualities, his nature has what she would have. Farther, when anything grows troublesome, recollect this maxim: This accident is not a misfortune, but bearing it well turns it to an advantage.

50. To consider those old people that resigned life so unwillingly, is a common yet not unserviceable aid in facing death. For what are these long-lived mortals more than those that went off in their infancy? What has become of Cadicianus, Fabius, Julianus, and Lepidus, and others like them? They buried a great many, but came at last to it themselves. Upon the whole, the difference between long and short life is insignificant, especially if you consider the accidents, the company, and the body you must go through with. Therefore do not let a thought of this kind affect you. Do but look upon the astonishing notion of time and eternity; what an immense deal has run out already, and how infinite it is still in the future. Do but consider this, and you will find three days and three ages of life come much to the same thing.

51. Always go the shortest way to work. Now,

the nearest road to your business is the road of nature. Let it be your constant method, then, to be sound in word and in deed, and by this means you need not grow fatigued, you need not quarrel, flourish, and dissemble like other people.

BOOK V.

BOOK V.

1. WHEN you find an unwillingness to rise early in the morning, make this short speech to yourself: I am getting up now to do the business of a man; and am I out of humour for going about that I was made for, and for the sake of which I was sent into the world? Was I then designed for nothing but to doze and keep warm beneath the counterpane? Well! but this is a comfortable way of living. Granting that: were you born only for pleasure? were you never to do anything? Is not action the end of your being? Pray look upon the plants and birds, the ants, spiders, and bees, and you will see them all exerting their nature, and busy in their station. Pray, shall not a man act like a man? Why do you not rouse your faculties, and hasten to act according to your nature? For all that, there is no living without rest. True; but nature has fixed a limit to eating and drinking, and here, too, you generally exceed bounds, and go beyond what is sufficient. Whereas in business you are apt to do less than lies in your power. In earnest, you have no true love for yourself. If you had, you would love your nature and

honour her wishes. Now, when a man loves his trade, how he will sweat and drudge to perform to perfection. But you honour your nature less than a turner does the art of turning, a dancing-master the art of dancing. And as for wealth and popularity, how eagerly are they pursued by the vain and the covetous? All these people when they greatly desire anything, seek to attain it, might and main, and will scarcely allow themselves necessary refreshment. And now, can you think the exercise of social duties less valuable than these petty amusements, and worth less exertion?

2. What an easy matter it is to stem the current of your imagination, to discharge a troublesome or improper thought, and at once return to a state of calm.

3. Do not think any word or action beneath you which is in accordance with nature; and never be misled by the apprehension of censure or reproach. Where honesty prompts you to say or do anything, never hold it beneath you. Other people have their own guiding principles and impulses; mind them not. Go on in the straight road, pursue your own and the common interest. For to speak strictly, these two are approached by one and the same road.

4. I will march on in the path of nature till my legs sink under me, and then I shall be at rest, and expire into that air which has given me my daily breath; fall upon that earth which has maintained my parents, helped my nurse to her milk, and supplied me with meat and drink for so many years; and though its favours have been often abused, still suffers me to tread upon it.

5. Wit and smartness are not your talent. What then? There are a great many other good qualities in which you cannot pretend nature has failed you; improve them as far as you can, and let us have that which is perfectly in your power. You may if you please behave yourself like a man of gravity and good faith, endure hardship, and despise pleasure; want but a few things, and complain of nothing; you may be gentle and magnanimous if you please, and have nothing of luxury or trifling in your disposition. Do not you see how much you may do if you have a mind to it, where the plea of incapacity is out of place? And yet you do not push forward as you should do. What then! Does any natural defect force you to grumble, to lay your faults upon your constitution, to be stingy or a flatterer, to seek after popularity, boast, and be disturbed in mind? Can you say you are so weakly made as to be driven to these practices? The immortal gods know the contrary. No, you might have stood clear of all this long since; and after all, if your parts were somewhat slow, and your understanding heavy, your way had been to have taken the more pains with yourself, and not to have lain fallow and remained content with your own dulness.

6. Some men, when they do you a kindness, at once demand the payment of gratitude from you; others are more modest than this. However, they remember the favour, and look upon you in a manner as their debtor. A third sort shall scarce know what they have done. These are much like a vine,

which is satisfied by being fruitful in its kind, and bears a bunch of grapes without expecting any thanks for it. A fleet horse or greyhound does not make a noise when they have done well, nor a bee neither when she has made a little honey. And thus a man that has done a kindness never proclaims it, but does another as soon as he can, just like a vine that bears again the next season. Now we should imitate those who are so obliging, as hardly to reflect on their beneficence. But you will say, a man ought not to act without reflection. It is surely natural for one that is generous to be conscious of his generosity; yes, truly, and to desire the person obliged should be sensible of it too. What you say is in a great measure true. But if you mistake my meaning, you will become one of those untoward benefactors I first mentioned; indeed, they too are misled by the plausibility of their reasoning. But if you will view the matter in its true colours, never fear that you will neglect any social act.

7. A prayer of the Athenians, "Send down, oh! send down rain, dear Zeus, on the ploughed fields and plains of the Athenians." Of a truth, we should not pray at all, or else in this simple and noble fashion.

8. Æsculapius, as we commonly say, has prescribed such an one riding out, walking in his slippers, or a cold bath. Now, with much the same meaning we may affirm that the nature of the universe has ordered this or that person a disease, loss of limbs or estate, or some such other calamity. For as in the first case, the word "prescribed" signifies a direc-

tion for the health of the patient, so in the latter it means an application fit for his constitution and fate. And thus these harsher events may be counted fit for us, as stone properly joined together in a wall or pyramid is said by the workmen to fit in. Indeed, the whole of nature consists of harmony. For as the world has its form and entireness from that universal matter of which it consists, so the character of fate results from the quality and concurrence of all other causes contained in it. The common people understand this notion very well. Their way of speaking is: "This happened to this man, therefore it was sent him and appointed for him." Let us then comply with our doom, as we do with the prescriptions of Æsculapius. These doses are often unpalatable and rugged, and yet the desire of health makes them go merrily down. Now that which nature esteems profit and convenience, should seem to you like your own health. And, therefore, when anything adverse happens, take it quietly to you; it is for the health of the universe, and the prosperity of Zeus himself. Depend upon it, this had never been sent you, if the universe had not found its advantage in it. Neither does nature act at random, or order anything which is not suitable to those beings under her government. You have two reasons, therefore, to be contented with your condition. *First*, because it has befallen you, and was appointed you from the beginning by the highest and most ancient causes. *Secondly*, The lot even of individuals is in a manner destined for the interest of him that governs the world. It perfects his nature in some measure, and causes and continues his happiness; for it holds in causes, no less than in parts of a whole that if you lop off any part of the continuity and connection, you maim the whole. Now, if you are displeased with your circumstances, you dismember nature, and pull the world in pieces, as much as lies in your power.

9. Be not uneasy, discouraged, or out of humour, because practice falls short of precept in some particulars. If you happen to be beaten, come on again, and be glad if most of your acts are worthy of human nature. Love that to which you return, and do not go like a schoolboy to his master, with an ill will. No, you must apply to philosophy with inclination, as those who have sore eyes make use of a good receipt. And when you are thus disposed, you will easily acquiesce in reason, and make your abode with her. And here you are to remember that philosophy will put you upon nothing but what your nature wishes and calls for. But you are crossing the inclinations of your nature. Is not this the most agreeable? And does not pleasure often deceive us under this pretence? Now think a little, and tell me what is there more delightful than greatness of mind, and generosity, simplicity, equanimity, and piety? And once more, what can be more delightful than prudence? than to be furnished with that faculty of knowledge and understanding which keeps a man from making a false step, and helps him to good fortune in all his business?

10. Things are so much perplexed and in the dark

that several great philosophers looked upon them as altogether unintelligible, and that there was no certain test for the discovery of truth. Even the Stoics agree that certainty is very hard to come at; that our assent is worth little, for where is infallibility to be found? However, our ignorance is not so great but that we may discover how transitory and insignificant all things are, and that they may fall into the worst hands. Farther, consider the temper of those you converse with, and you will find the best will hardly do; not to mention that a man has work enough to make himself tolerable to himself. And since we have nothing but darkness and dirt to grasp at, since time and matter, motion and mortals are in perpetual flux; for these reasons, I say, I cannot imagine what there is here worth the minding or being eager about. On the other hand, a man ought to keep up his spirits, for it will not be long before his discharge comes. In the meantime, he must not fret at the delay, but satisfy himself with these two considerations: the one is, that nothing will befall me but what is in accordance with the nature of the universe; the other, that I need do nothing contrary to my mind and divinity, since no one can force me to act thus, or force me to act against my own judgment.

11. What use do I put my soul to? It is a serviceable question this, and should frequently be put to oneself. How does my ruling part stand affected? And whose soul have I now? That of a child, or a young man, or a feeble woman, or of a tyrant, of cattle or wild beasts.

12. What sort of good things those are, which are commonly so reckoned, you may learn from hence. For the purpose, if you reflect upon those qualities which are intrinsically valuable, such as prudence, temperance, justice, and fortitude, you will not find it possible afterwards to give ear to those, for this is not suitable to a good man. But if you have once conceived as good what appears so to the many, you will hear and gladly accept as suitable the saying of the comic writer. Thus we see the generality are struck with the distinction, otherwise they would not dislike the liberty in one case, and allow it in the other, holding it a suitable and witty jest when it is directed against wealth, and the means that further luxury and ambition. Now, what significancy and excellence can there be in these things, to which may be applied the poet's jest, that excess of luxury leaves no room for comfort?

13. My being consists of matter and form, that is, of soul and body; annihilation will reach neither of them, for they were never produced out of nothing. The consequence is, that every part of me will serve to make something in the world; and this again will change into another part through an infinite succession of change. This constant method of alteration gave me my being, and my father before me, and so on to eternity backward: for I think I may speak thus, even though the world be confined within certain determinate periods.

14. Reason and the reasoning faculty need no foreign assistance, but are sufficient for their own pur-

poses. They move within themselves, and make directly for the point in view. Wherefore, acts in accordance with them are called right acts, for they lead along the right road.

15. Those things do not belong to a man which do not belong to him as a man. For they are not included in the idea; they are not required of us as men; human nature does not promise them, neither is it perfected by them. From whence it follows that they can neither constitute the chief end of man, nor strictly contribute towards it. Farther, if these things were any real additions, how comes the contempt of them, and the being easy without them, to be so great a commendation? To balk an advantage would be folly if these things were truly good. But the case stands otherwise; for we know that self-denial and indifference about these things, and patience when they are taken away, is the character of a good man.

16. Your manners will depend very much upon the quality of what you frequently think on; for the soul is as it were tinged with the colour and complexion of thought. Be sure therefore to work in such maxims as these. Wherever a man lives, he may live well; by consequence, a life of virtue and that of a courtier are not inconsistent. Again, that which a thing is made for, is that towards which it is carried, and in that which it is naturally carried to, lies the end of the act. Now where the end of a thing is, there the advantage and improvement of it is certainly lodged. Now the happiness of mankind lies in society, since

that we were made for this purpose, I have proved already. For is it not plain that the lower order of beings are made for the higher, and the higher for the service of each other? Now as those with souls are superior to the soulless, so amongst all creatures with souls the rational are the best.

17. To expect an impossibility is madness. Now it is impossible for ill men not to do ill.

18. There is nothing happens to any person but what was in his power to go through with. Some people have had very severe trials, and yet either by having less understanding, or more pride than ordinary, have charged bravely through the misfortune, and come off without a scratch. Now it is a disgrace to let ignorance and vanity do more with us than prudence and principle.

19. Outward objects cannot take hold of the soul, nor force their passage into her, nor set any of her wheels going. No, the impression comes from herself, and it is her own motions which affect her. As for the contingencies of fortune, they are either great or little, according to the opinion she has of her own strength.

20. When we consider we are bound to be serviceable to mankind, and bear with their faults, we shall perceive there is a common tie of nature and relation between us. But when we see people grow troublesome and disturb us in our business, here we are to look upon men as indifferent sort of things, no less than sun or wind, or a wild beast. It is true they may hinder me in the executing part, but all this is of

no moment while my inclinations and good intent stand firm, for these can act according to the condition and change. For the mind converts and changes every hindrance into help. And thus it is probable I may gain by the opposition, and let the obstacle help me on my road.

21. Among all things in the universe, direct your worship to the greatest. And which is that? It is that being which manages and governs all the rest. And as you worship the best thing in nature, so you are to pay a proportionate regard to the best thing in yourself, and this is akin to the Deity. The quality of its functions will discover it. It is the reigning power within you, which disposes of your actions and your fortune.

22. That which does not hurt the city or body politic cannot hurt the citizen. Therefore when you think you are ill-used, let this reflection be your remedy: If the community is not the worse for it, neither am I. But if the community is injured, your business is to show the person concerned his fault, but not to grow passionate about it.

23. Reflect frequently upon the instability of things, and how very fast the scenes of nature are shifted. Matter is in a perpetual flux. Change is always and everywhere at work; it strikes through causes and effects, and leaves nothing fixed and permanent. And then how very near us stand the two vast gulfs of time, the past and the future, in which all things disappear. Now is not that man a blockhead that lets these momentary things make him

proud, or uneasy, or sorrowful, as though they could trouble him for long?

24. Remember what an atom your person is in respect of the universe, what a minute of immeasurable time falls to your share, and what a small concern you are in the empire of fate!

25. A man misbehaves himself towards me; what is that to me? The action is his, and the disposition that led him to it is his, and therefore let him look to it. As for me, I am in the condition the universal nature assigns me, and am doing what my own nature assigns me.

26. Whether the motions of your body are rugged or agreeable, do not let your ruling and governing principle be concerned with them; confine the impressions to their respective quarters, and let your mind keep her distance, and not mingle with them. It is true, that which results from the laws of the union through the force of sympathy or constitution, must be felt, for nature will have its course. But though the sensation cannot be stopped, it must not be overrated, nor strained to the quality of good or evil.

27. We ought to live with the gods. This is done by him who always exhibits a soul contented with the appointments of Providence, and obeys the orders of that divinity which is his deputy and ruler, and the offspring of God. Now this divine authority is neither more nor less than that soul and reason which every man possesses.

28. Are you angry at a rank smell or an ill-scented

breath? What good will this anger do you? But you will say, the man has reason, and can, if he takes pains, discover wherein he offends. I wish you joy of your discovery. Well, if you think mankind so full of reason, pray make use of your own. Argue the case with the faulty person, and show him his error. If your advice prevails, he is what you would have him; and then there is no need of being angry.

29. You may live now if you please, as you would choose to do if you were near dying. But suppose people will not let you, why then, give life the slip, but by no means make a misfortune of it. If the room smokes I leave it, and there is an end, for why should one be concerned at the matter? However, as long as nothing of this kind drives me out, I stay, behave as a free man, and do what I have a mind to; but then I have a mind to nothing but what I am led to by reason and public interest.

30. The soul of the universe is of a social disposition. For this reason it has made the lower part of the creation for the sake of the higher. And as for those beings of the higher rank, it has bound them to each other. You see how admirably things are ranged and subordinated according to the dignity of their kind, and cemented together in mutual harmony.

31. Recollect how you have behaved yourself all along towards the gods, your parents, brothers, wife, and children; towards your instructors, governors, friends, acquaintance, and servants. Whether men can say of you, "He never wronged a man in word or deed." Recollect how much business you have been

engaged in, and what you have had strength to endure; that now your task is done, and the history of your life finished. Remember likewise, how many fair sights you have seen, how much of pleasure and pain you have despised, how much glory disregarded, and how often you have done good against evil.

32. Why should skill and knowledge be disturbed at the censures of ignorance? But who are these knowing and skilful people? Why, those who are acquainted with the original cause and end of all things, with that reason that pervades the mass of matter, renews the world at certain periods, and governs it through all the lengths of time.

33. You will quickly be reduced to ashes and skeleton. And it may be you will have a name left you, and it may be not. And what is a name? Nothing but sound and echo. And then for those things which are so much valued in the world, they are miserably empty and rotten, and insignificant. It is like puppies snarling for a bone; and the contests of little children sometimes transported, and then again all in tears about a plaything. And as for modesty and good faith, truth and justice, they have fled "up to Olympus from the wide-spread earth." And now, what is it that can keep you here? For if the objects of sense are floating and changeable, and the organs misty, and apt to be imposed on; if the soul is but a vapour drawn off the blood, and the applause of little mortals insignificant; if the case stands thus, why not have patience till you are either

extinguished or removed? And till that time comes, what is to be done? The answer is easy: to worship the gods, and speak honourably of them; to be beneficial to mankind; to bear with them or avoid them; and lastly, to remember that whatever lies without the compass of your own flesh and breath is nothing of yours, nor in your power.

34. You may be always successful if you do but set out well, and let your thoughts and practice proceed upon right method. There are two properties and privileges common to the soul of God and man and all rational beings. The one is, not to be hindered by anything external; the other, to make virtuous intention and action their supreme satisfaction, and not so much as to desire anything farther.

35. If this accident is no fault of mine, nor a consequence of it; and besides, if the community is never the worse for it, why am I concerned? Now, how is the community injured?

36. Do not suffer a sudden impression to overbear your judgment. Let those that want your assistance have it, as far as the case requires. But if they are injured in matters indifferent, do not consider it any real damage, for that is a bad habit. But as the old man, when he went away, asked back his foster-child's top, remembering that it was a top, so do in this case also. When you are haranguing in the rostra, a little of this to yourself would not be amiss:—Hark you, friend, have you forgotten what this glitter of honour really is? I grant it is but tinsel, but for all that it is extremely valued. And because other people are fools, must

you be so too? I can at once become happy anywhere, for he is happy who has found for himself a happy lot. In a word, happiness lies all in the functions of reason, in warrantable desires and virtuous practice.

BOOK VI.

BOOK VI.

1. AS the substance of the universe is pliable and obedient, so that sovereign reason which gives laws to it has neither motive nor inclination to bring an evil upon anything. It has no evil in its nature, nor does evil, but forms and governs all things, and hurts nothing.

2. Do but your duty, and do not trouble yourself, whether it is in the cold, or by a good fire, whether you are overwatched, or satisfied with sleep, whether you have a good word or a bad one, whether you are dying, or doing anything else, for this last must be done at one time or other. It is part of the business of life to leave it, and here too it suffices to manage the present well.

3. Look thoroughly into matters, and let not the peculiar quality or intrinsic value of anything escape you.

4. The present appearance of things will quickly undergo a change, and be either exhaled into common matter or dispersed.

5. That intelligent Being that governs the universe has perfect views of His own nature and acts, and of the matter on which He acts.

6. The best way of revenge is not to imitate the injury.

7. Be always doing something serviceable to mankind, and let this constant generosity be your only pleasure, not forgetting in the meantime a due regard to the Deity.

8. The governing part of the mind arouses and alters itself; gives what air it pleases to its own likeness, and to all the accidents and circumstances without.

9. The particular effects in the world are all wrought by one intelligent nature. This universal cause has no foreign assistant, no interloping principle, either without or within it.

10. The world is either a medley of atoms that now intermingle and now are scattered apart, or else it is a unity under the laws of order and providence. If the first, what should I stay for, where nature is in such a chaos, and things are so blindly jumbled together? Why do I care for anything else than to return to the element of earth as soon as may be? Why should I give myself any trouble? Let me do what I will, my elements will be scattered. But if there is a Providence, then I adore the great Governor of the world, and am easy and of good cheer in the prospect of protection.

11. When you happen to be ruffled a little by any untoward accident, retire immediately into your reason, and do not move out of tune any further than needs must; for the sooner you return to harmony, the more you will get it in your own power.

12. Put the case, you had a step-mother and a mother at the same time; though you would pay a regard to the first, your converse, I conceive, would be mostly with the latter. Let the court and philosophy represent these two relations to you; apply frequently to this last, and seek your refreshment with her. For it is a life of virtue and philosophy which makes life at court tolerable to you, and you yourself tolerable.

13. When we have meat before us, or other dishes, we receive the impression that this is but the carcass of a fish, this of a fowl, and the other of a pig. And then for this bottle of Falernian, what is it but a little moisture squeezed out of the berry of a grape? And your purple is nothing but sheep's hair twisted together, and stained in the gore of a little shell-fish. And if we were to proceed to some other satisfactions of sense, we should find them but coarse in their causes and constitution; and as these notions strike through the surface, press into the heart of things, and shew them in their natural colours, so we should carry them on, and apply them to all the pageantry of life. And where things appear most plausible, be sure to bring them to the test, and look at their worthlessness, and strip them of all the words by which they were exalted. Without this care, figure and appearance are great cheats; and when you think your fancy is best employed, you will be most fooled. Remember what Crates said even of Xenocrates.

14. The inclination of the generality may be reduced to these heads: Some people are little enough

to be attracted by things in the state of bare existence or vegetation, as with stones, wood, figs, grapes, olives, and such like. Others, who are somewhat more reasonable in their fancy, must have life to charm them; and these, it may be, are in love with their flocks and herds. A third sort, better furnished than the former, admire nothing beneath a rational soul, and this not as a whole, but as it were they pride themselves in slaves, possessed of some skill, parts, or industry. But he that values a rational creature that is social and universal runs into none of the follies above mentioned, but makes it his chief business to look to his own soul, and keep it in rational and social movements, and to assist all mankind in the public interest.

15. Some things are pressing into being, and others are hastening out of it, and that which was entire just now, is part of it spent already. The world is renewed by this change and flux, no less than the infinite series of ages by the perpetual succession of time. Now, who would set a value upon things hurried thus fast down the stream, on which it is impossible to stop? Such a passion is much like falling in love with a sparrow flying over your head. You have, as it were, but one glimpse of her, and she is out of sight. Life is but a sort of exhalation of the blood, and a little breathing in of air. Now, to inhale and exhale your breath for the support of life, which you do every moment, and expire your last, when you lose the whole power of breathing which you received at your birth yesterday or the day before, is much the same action.

16. Neither the perspiration of plants, nor the breath of animals, nor the impressions of sensation, nor the puppet-motions of passions are privileges of any great value. To which we may add the instinct of crowding into herds, together with the functions of nutrition, this latter being not unlike a separating of our food. What then is it that you count worth your esteem? Applause? Not at all. Why, then, you must not value the applause of tongues, for the commendation of the multitude is nothing else. Well, I find fame and glory will not tempt you; what, then, is there behind worth the having? To govern your motions, and make use of your being according to the intentions of nature. This is the design of arts and improvement in other cases, every artificer and profession endeavouring to make the thing fit to answer the end for which it was intended. This, for instance, is the design of vine-dressers and those that manage horses and dogs. And learning and education have all one object in view. It is agreed then, the main point lies here. Compass but this, and let all things else alone. Must your inclinations always run riot, and will you never become free, self-contained, and passionless? This temper will let loose abundance of uneasy passions upon you. It will make you grow envious, full of jealousy and suspicion, and apt to overreach those who are possessed of something you have a mind to. And when strong desires are unsatisfied, you will find yourself mightily disturbed. And this will make you murmur and grow mutinous against the gods. But if you come once to pay a due

regard and reverence to your own reason, you will be pleased with yourself, serviceable to society, and compliant with the gods. That is, you will be entirely satisfied with their rule and administration.

17. The elements either press upwards, or fall downwards, or else run round in a circle. But virtue has none of these motions ; she is of a nobler kind. Her progress in regular thoughts is somewhat unintelligible, but always prosperous.

18. What a strange humour there is amongst some people. They do not care to afford a good word to their contemporaries, and yet are very desirous of being praised by posterity, that is, by those they never saw, nor ever will have the least acquaintance with. Now this is almost as absurd as it would be to be disturbed because you were not commended by the generations that lived before you.

19. Because you find a thing very difficult, do not at once conclude that no man can master it. But whatever you observe proper and practicable by another, believe likewise within your own power.

20. If an antagonist in the circus tears our flesh with his nails, or tilts against us with his head, and wounds us, we do not cry out foul play, nor are we offended at the rough usage, nor suspect him afterwards as a dangerous person in conversation. It is true, when we are at the exercise we guard and parry, but all this is done without raising ill blood, or looking upon the man as an enemy. Let us act in this way in the other instances of life. When we receive a blow, let us disregard it, thinking we are but at a

trial of skill, for, as I said before, it is in our power to retire without feeling malice and ill-will.

21. If any one can convince me of an error, I shall be very glad to change my opinion, for truth is my business, and nobody was ever yet hurt by it. No; he that continues in ignorance and mistake, it is he that receives the mischief.

22. I do my duty, that is enough. As for other things, I shall never be disturbed about them. For they are either without life or without reason, or they have lost their way and cannot find it.

23. As for brute animals, and things undignified with reason, use them generously and nobly, as beings that have reason should treat those that have none. But treat men, since they have reason, as members of the same society. And in all your affairs invoke the gods for their assistance. As for the time you are to continue this, never trouble yourself whether it is long or short. For three hours of life thus well spent are sufficient.

24. Alexander the Great and his groom, when dead, were both upon the same level, and ran the same chance of being scattered into atoms or absorbed in the soul of the universe.

25. What abundance of motions there are in the body, what abundance of thoughts in the mind at the same time! He that considers this will not wonder so much that infinitely more productions, nay rather, all that are, should exist together in that great whole we call the universe.

26. Suppose you were asked to spell Antoninus's

name, would you sound every letter with emphasis in the company's ears? Or would you return their passion if they were angry? I conceive you would rather go mildly to work, and give them the letters and syllables as they stand, without noise. Apply this to greater instances, and remember that all duties in morality have a determinate number of parts to render them complete. These must be observed, and performed in order; but it must be done smoothly, without growing provoked upon meeting with provocation.

27. You hold it cruel to balk people's fancies, and not give them leave to pursue what they reckon their interest. Yet with this you are chargeable in some measure yourself when you are angry with those that do amiss; for they are carried towards what they esteem their own interest and convenience. But that you will say is their mistake. Then it is your part to lead them out of it, and to show them their error without resentment.

28. What is death? It is a resting from the vibrations of sensation, and the swayings of desire, a stop upon the rambling of thought, and a release from the drudgery about your body.

29. It would be a shame if your mind should falter and give in before your body.

30. Have a care you have not too much of a Cæsar in you, and that you are not dyed with that dye. This is easily learned, therefore guard against the infection. Be candid, virtuous, sincere, and modestly grave. Let justice and piety have their share in your

character; let your temper be remarkable for mildness and affection, and be always enterprising and vigorous in your business. And, in short, strive to be just such a man as virtue and philosophy meant you to be. Worship the gods and protect mankind. This life is short, and all the advantage you can get by it is a pious disposition and unselfish acts. Do everything as a disciple of Antoninus; imitate him in the vigour and constancy of his good conduct, in the equality, sweetness, and piety of his temper, the serenity of his aspect, his contempt of fame, and the generous ambition he had to be perfectly master of his business. Further, it was his way to dismiss nothing till he had looked through it, and viewed it on all sides; to bear unreasonable remonstrances without making a return; never to be in a hurry; to be backward in giving encouragement to informers. He was a great judge of men and manners, but of no reprimanding humour; not at all apt to be frighted; not too suspicious, nor like a sophist. Satisfied with a little, as one might easily perceive by his palace, his furniture, his habit, his eating, and his attendance. His disposition was patient, and fatigueing his delight. He was temperate in his diet. He was firm in his friendship, and steady and agreeable in the manner of showing it. He gave his courtiers all the freedom imaginable to contradict him, and was pleased with the proposal of a better expedient than his own. To conclude, he was a religious prince, but without superstition. Pray imitate these good qualities of his, that you may have the satisfaction of them at your last hour as he had.

31. Rouse and recollect yourself, and you will perceive your trouble lay only in a scene of imagination. And when you are well awake, look upon these realities as you did upon those visions.

32. My person consists of soul and a little body. To this latter all things are morally indifferent, the body being in no condition to make a distinction of this kind. And as to my mind, there is nothing can affect her, her own actions excepted; now these are all within her power, and of all her actions she is only concerned with the present, for what is past or to come, signifies as much as nothing, and is at present indifferent.

33. As long as the hands and feet do the work they were made for, they move naturally, and with ease. Thus while a man performs the functions of a man, and keeps true to his condition, he feels no more weight than what nature lays upon him. Now that which is not beside the intentions of nature can never be a real misfortune.

34. What abundance of sensual satisfaction have thieves, parricides, and usurpers been possessed of?

35. Do not you observe among your artificers, though they bear the contradiction and impertinence of the unskilful, yet they will not comply so far as to be talked out of their knowledge, or work against the rules of their trade? And is it not a scandalous business, that an architect or a physician should have more regard for his profession than a man has for his? For his, I say, in which he has the honour of the gods for his partners.

36. The vast continents of Europe and Asia are but corners of the creation. The ocean is but a drop, and Mount Athos but a grain in respect of the universe, and the present time but a point to the extent of eternity. These things have all of them petty, changeable, and transitory beings. Remember likewise that all things proceed from the soul of the universe, either by direct or indirect causality. Thus the growling deformity of a lion, the poison of serpents, and whatever seems offensive in nature, as thorns or dirt, are the outcome of something noble and beautiful. Do not therefore suppose them insignificant and unworthy the being you worship, but consider the fountain whence all things spring.

37. He that has taken a view of the present age, has seen as much as if he had begun with the world, and gone to the end of it; for all things are of one kind and of one form.

38. The mutual dependence all things have, and the relation they stand in to each other, is worth your frequent observation. For all the parts of matter are in some measure linked together and interwoven, and for this reason have a natural sympathy for each other. For one thing comes in order after another, and this comes about through their active movement and harmony, and the unity of their substance.

39. Bring your will to your fate, and suit your mind to your circumstances, and love those people heartily that it is your fortune to be engaged with.

40. Those tools, vessels, and utensils are said to be right, which serve for the uses they were made, though

in this case the artificer that made them is commonly absent. But in the works of nature, the forming power is always present with the effect, and abides there, wherefore this deserves a particular regard. From hence you are to conclude that as long as you behave yourself as this sovereign power directs you, you will live in accordance with intelligence. In this way too all things in the universe are directed by intelligence.

41. If you suppose anything which lies out of your command to be good or evil, your missing the one or falling into the other will unavoidably make you a malcontent against the gods, and cause you to hate those people whom you either know or suspect to be instrumental in your misfortune. To be plain, our being concerned for these objects often makes us very unreasonable and unjust. But if we confine the notion of good and evil to things in our power, then all the motives to complaint will drop off; then we shall neither remonstrate against Heaven, nor quarrel with any mortal living.

42. All people work in some measure towards the ends of Providence, some with knowledge and design, though others are not sensible of it. And thus, as I remember, Heraclitus observes, that those who are asleep may be said to help the world forward. In short, the grand design is carried on by different hands and different means. For even he that complaining makes head against his fate, and strives to pull the administration in pieces, even such a testy mortal as this contributes his share abundantly, for the universe

had need even of such an one. Consider, then, how you are ranging yourself, and what workers you are joining. For He that governs the world will certainly make you good for something, and prove serviceable to his scheme, one way or other. Have a care you do not make such a ridiculous figure in nature, as that mean and ridiculous verse did in the play Chrysippus mentions.

43. The sun never covets the properties of a shower, nor does Æsculapius interfere with the fruit-bearing god. Are not the stars different from each other? And yet their influences work towards the same end.

44. If the gods have decreed anything concerning me or my business, they have decreed my advantage. For it is absurd to suppose that they are mistaken in their measures, or not benevolent in their design. For to what purpose should they intend me any harm? What would themselves, or the universe, the special object of their providence, gain by it? But granting they have made no particular provision for me, yet since their government of the world is not disputed, the consequence will be much the same. And why, then, should I not be contented with whatever happens as a consequence of the universal whole? To put the case further. Suppose the gods take care of nothing (which, by the way, we must reckon a scandalous opinion), then it will be high time to leave off the common solemnities of sacrificing, prayers and religious swearing, and all those observances which we keep as though the gods were present and dwelling with us. If the

gods, therefore, will take care of none of us, it is certainly lawful for me to take care of myself. Now, it is my right to consider my own convenience, and what is that? Why, that is convenient for every one, which suits his nature and his constitution. Now reason and social principles are suited to my nature. Take me, then, under the particular distinction of Antoninus, and Rome is my town and country; but consider me as a man in general, and I belong to the corporation of the world. That, therefore, and only that which is serviceable to both these societies, is an advantage to me.

45. Whatever happens to particulars, is serviceable to the universe, that thought might satisfy. But we can carry the reasons for acquiescence farther, for upon observation you will perceive that what is profitable to one man, is in some measure for the interest of the rest. And here I take the word profit in the common meaning of things neither good nor bad.

46. You may remember that at a play, or such like diversion, the same thing coming over and over again tires the sense, and extinguishes the pleasure. Remove this contemplation into life; for here all things come round, and bring the same causes and appearances along with them. How long, then, will this last?

47. Consider with yourself that people of all conditions, professions, and countries are dead, if you cast your eyes back as far as Philistion, Phœbus, or Origanion. Now turn towards the other classes of men. And we must take our turn, too, with the rest,

and remove to the same place whither so many famous orators and great philosophers, such as Heraclitus, Pythagoras, and Socrates have shown us the way. So many heroes and generals and princes, and besides Eudoxus, Hipparchus, and Archimedes, not to mention a great many other extraordinary geniuses, persons of industry, wit, spirit, and versatility and confidence; they are all gone; even those buffoons, who, like Menippus, mocked at this perishable and transitory existence. Remember they are all in their graves. And where is the harm of all this? nay, what are those the worse for it, that have not so much as left their own names behind them? In a word, there is only one thing here worth the minding, and that is, to be true and just, and to show benevolence, even to the untrue and unjust.

48. When you have a mind to divert your fancy, consider the good qualities of your acquaintance; as the enterprising vigour of this man, the modesty of another, the liberality of a third, and so on. For there is nothing so entertaining as a lively image of the virtues exhibited in the character of those we converse with, occurring as numerously as possible. Let this, therefore, be always at hand.

49. You are not angry because you weigh so light in the scale, and do not ride forty stone. Why, then, should you be dissatisfied because your life is not drawn out to an unusual and extraordinary period? You ought to be no more covetous of time than you are of bulk, but be contented with your own allowance.

50. It is good to try to bring people to a right

understanding of the case; but if they are unwilling, be governed by the law of justice. If there comes a force upon you and stops your progress, abandon it and be easy, and make a virtue of necessity. Remember that you undertook the business upon the condition of its being feasible, and never pretended to grasp at impossibilities. What was it, then, you aimed at? Why, to do your best in your effort. Right! And this may be effectually done, though the enterprise should happen to miscarry.

51. The ambitious person lodges his happiness in the activity of another, the voluptuary in his own affections, but a man of understanding places his good in his own action.

52. We are at liberty not to misinterpret any accident, and by consequence may be free from disturbance. Things have no natural power over thoughts to influence our judgment.

53. Accustom yourself to attend to what is discoursed, and as far as you can get into the soul of him that speaks.

54. That which is not for the interest of the whole swarm is not for the interest of a single bee.

55. If the patient rails at the doctor, or the crew at the master of the vessel, whom will they mind, or how can the doctor secure their health, or the master of the vessel a good voyage?

56. How many people that came into the world with me are gone out of it already?

57. Honey tastes bitter to the jaundiced, and people bitten by a mad dog are frightened at the sight

of water. And on the other hand, a little ball is a beautiful thing to a child. This considered, why should you be angry with any one? Can you imagine that error has less force upon the mind than a little bile or poison upon the body?

58. As nobody can rob you of the privileges of your nature, or force you to live counter to your reason, so nothing can happen to you but what is consistent with the interest of the universe.

59. Consider with yourself what sort of people men must court, and for what base objects and by what scandalous actions. And then how time will cover all things, and how many it has covered already.

BOOK VII.

BOOK VII.

1. WHAT is wickedness? What you have often seen. When you are in danger of being shocked, consider that the sight is nothing but what you have frequently seen already. Everywhere up and down, ages and histories, towns and families, are full of the same stories. There is nothing new to be met with; but all things are common, and quickly over.

2. Opinions, whether right or wrong, can never be pulled out of your head, unless the impressions on which they rest are first removed. It is in your power to kindle them afresh, or to form a right judgment upon the present emergency. And why, then, should I be disturbed at it? For nothing that does not enter my mind, and get within me, can hurt me. Hold to this, and you are safe. Come, I will tell you a way how you may live your time over again. Do but recollect, and review what you have seen already, and the work is done.

3. Gazing after shows, the diversions of the stage, farms well stocked with flocks and herds, contests for victory in the field are all much the same. So, too, a

bone thrown to puppies, fishes scrambling for a bait, ants laboriously carrying a grain of wheat, mice frighted out of their wits and running away, puppets danced upon a wire. And in the midst of them a wise man must be good-humoured, and not grow haughty in the contemplation. Remembering, notwithstanding, that the true worth of a man is to be measured by the objects he pursues.

4. Do not let either discourse or action pass unobserved; attend to the sense and signification of the one, and to the tendency and design of the other.

5. Is my intellect sufficient for this business or not? If it is, I will make use of my talent as given me by heaven for that purpose. If not, I will either let it alone, and resign it to a better capacity, unless that be contrary to my duty, or else I will do what I can. I will give my advice, and put the executing part into an abler hand, and thus the right moment and the general interest may be secured. For whatsoever I act, either by myself, or in conjunction with another, I am always to aim at the advantage of the community.

6. How many famous men are dropped out of history and forgotten? And how many, that promised to keep up other people's names, have lost their own?

7. Never be ashamed of assistance. Like a soldier at the storming of a town, your business is to maintain your post, and execute your orders. Now suppose you happen to be lame at an assault, and cannot mount the breach upon your own feet, will you not suffer your comrade to help you?

8. Be not disturbed about the future, for if ever you come to it, you will have the same reason for your guide, which preserves you at present.

9. All parts of the universe are interwoven and tied together with a sacred bond. And no one thing is foreign or unrelated to another. This general connection gives unity and ornament to the world. For the world, take it altogether, is but one. There is but one sort of matter to make it of; one God that pervades it; and one law to guide it, the common reason of all rational beings; and one truth; if, indeed, beings of the same kind, and endued with the same reason, have one and the same perfection.

10. Everything material quickly disappears into the universal matter. And everything causal is quickly absorbed into the universal reason. And the memory of everything is quickly overwhelmed by time.

11. With rational beings action in accordance with nature and reason is the same thing.

12. Either stand upright upon your own legs, or upon your crutches.

13. Just as connection creates sympathy in the members of the body, so relation of nature does the same thing among rational beings. For though separate in space, they seem all made to co-operate with each other. This thought will be more intelligible and affecting, if you frequently consider yourself as a member of the rational system. But if you reckon yourself only a part, you do not yet love mankind with all your heart. A generous action does not yet delight you from con-

viction; you do a good office merely for fashion and decency, but not as if it were really a kindness to yourself.

14. Let accidents happen to such as are liable to the impression, and those that feel misfortune may complain of it, if they please. As for me, let what will come, I can receive no damage by it, unless I think it a calamity; and it is in my power to think it none, if I have a mind to it.

15. Let people's tongues and actions be what they will, my business is to be good. And make the same speech to myself, that a piece of gold, or an emerald, or purple should. Let people talk and act as they please; I must be an emerald, and I must keep my colour.

16. Does the mind ever cause herself disturbance? Does she bring fears and passions upon herself? Let any other body try to frighten or trouble her if they can, for of her own conviction she will not turn to such impressions. And as for this small carcass, let it take care not to feel, and if it does, say so. But the soul, the seat of passion and pain, which forms an opinion on these things, need suffer nothing, unless she throws herself into these fancies and fears. For the mind is in her own nature self-sufficient, and must create her wants before she can feel them. This privilege makes her undisturbed and above restraint, unless she teazes and puts fetters upon herself.

17. Happiness is the possession of a good genius or goodness. Why then does fancy break in and disturb the scene? Begone! by the gods, as you

came; I do not want you! However, since you have custom to plead in your excuse, withdraw, and I will forgive you.

18. Is anyone afraid of change? I would gladly know what can be done without it? and what is dearer and more suitable to the universal nature? Pray, must not your wood be transformed before your bath can be ready for you? Must not your meat be changed to make it fit to nourish you? Indeed, what part of life or convenience can go forward without alteration? Now, in all likelihood a change in your condition may be as serviceable to the world in general, as those alterations above mentioned are to you.

19. All particular bodies are hurried as through a swift torrent through the universal mass of which they are incorporate, like a sort of serviceable limbs to the world. How many a Chrysippus, Socrates, and Epictetus have sunk in the gulf of time? And the same reflection will hold good concerning any other person or thing whatsoever.

20. I am only solicitous about one thing, and that is, lest I should do something that the constitution of man does not permit, or in the way or time it does not permit.

21. It will not be long before you will have forgotten all the world, and in a little time all the world will forget you too.

22. It is the privilege of human nature to love those that disoblige us. To practise this, you must consider that the offending party is of kin to you, that ignorance is the cause of the misbehaviour, and the

fault is involuntary, that you will both of you quickly be in your graves; but especially consider that you have received no harm by the injury, for your mind is never the worse for it.

23. The universal nature works the universal matter like wax. Now for the purpose, it is a horse; soon after you will have it melted down, and run into the figure of a tree, then a man, then something else. And it is but a little while that it is fixed in one species. Now a trunk feels no more pain by being knocked in pieces than when it was first put together.

24. A sour gruff look is very unnatural, and to put it on often will make it settle, and destroy the beauty and pleasantness of the aspect to that degree that it is never to be recovered: from whence you may conclude it is a foolish custom. It is high time for those people to die that have outlived the sense of their own misdemeanours.

25. That being which governs nature will quickly change the present face of it. One thing will be made out of another by frequent revolutions. And thus the world will be always new.

26. When anyone misbehaves himself towards you, immediately bethink yourself what notions he has concerning advantage and disadvantage. When you have found out this, you will pity him, and neither be angry nor surprised at the matter. It may be upon enquiry you may find your opinions upon these points much the same, and then you ought to pardon him. But if your notions of good and evil are different, then you will more easily bear with his ignorance.

27. Do not let your head run upon that which is none of your own, but pick out some of the best of your circumstances, and consider how eagerly you would wish for them, were they not in your possession; but then you must take care to keep your satisfaction within compass, for fear it should carry you too far, make you over-value the object, and be disturbed at the loss of it.

28. Rely upon yourself, for it is the nature of the principle that rules within us, to be satisfied with honesty, and the inward quiet consequent to it.

29. Rub out the colours of imagination. Do not suffer your passions to make a puppet of you. Confine your care to the present. Look through that which happens either to yourself or another. Distinguish the parts of your subject, and divide them into the causal and material element. Think upon your last hour, and do not trouble yourself about other people's faults, but leave them with those that must answer for them.

30. When you hear a discourse, make your understanding keep pace with it, and reach as far as you can into events and their causes.

31. Would you set off your person, and recommend yourself? Let it be done by simplicity, by modesty of behaviour, and by indifference to things neither good nor bad. Love mankind and resign to providence. For as the poet observes, "All things are under law," not the elements only, but it suffices to remember that there are at the most but very few things in the world that are not under law.

32. Concerning death: It is a dispersion if there

are atoms; but if the universe is a unity, it is either extinction or change.

33. As for pain, if it is intolerable it will quickly dispatch you. If it stays long it is bearable. Your mind in the meantime preserves herself calm by the strength of the opining faculty, and suffers nothing. And for your limbs that are hurt by the pain, if they can complain, let them do it.

34. As for fame, consider the intellect of the people that are to commend, how insignificant they are, and how little in their pursuits and aversions. Consider also that as one heap of sand thrown upon another covers the first, so it happens in life, a new glory soon eclipses an old one.

35. A saying of Plato, "He that has raised his mind to a due pitch of greatness, that has carried his view through the whole extent of matter and time, do you imagine such an one will think much of human life? Not at all (says the other man in the dialogue). What then? Will the fear of death afflict him? Far from it."

36. Antisthenes said, "It is a royal thing to be ill spoken of for good deeds."

37. It is a shame that a man should be master of his countenance, and compose or control it as the mind directs, while that mind is not controlled by itself.

38. "Ne'er fret at accidents, for things are sullen,
And don't regard your anger."

39. "To the immortal gods and us give joy."

40. "Fate mows down life like corn, this mortal falls;
The other stands awhile."

41. "If I and mine are by the gods neglected,
There's reason for their rigour."

42. "For the good is with me and the just."

43. "No joining others in their wailing, no violent emotion."

44. More of Plato's sentences:—"To such a one I should return this very reasonable answer, Hark ye, friend, you are mightily out if you think a man that is good for anything is either afraid of living or dying. No; his concern is only whether in doing anything he is doing right or wrong—acting the part of a good man or a bad."

45. Plato again:—"In my opinion, when a man holds a post with his own choice, or has been put into it by his superior, his business is to remain there in the hour of danger, and fear nothing but disgrace and cowardice."

46. Plato once more:—"With your favour, sir, it is not always the part of virtue and bravery to preserve either your own life or your neighbour's. He that is a man in good earnest must not be so mean as to whine for life, and grasp intemperately at old age: let him leave this point to Providence. The women can tell him that we must go when our time is come. His duty is to consider how he may make the most of his life, and spend what there is to the best advantage."

47. Consider the course of the stars as if you were driving through the sky with them. Let the transmutation of the elements be frequently the subject of your meditation. Such contemplations as these scour off the rust contracted by dwelling here below.

48. It is a fine saying that of Plato's:—"That when we consider the state and condition of mankind, we should place our imagination upon some lofty pyramid, and from thence take a prospect of the world, and look it over as it were at one view. Here we may see flocks, armies, husbandry, marriages and separations, births and deaths, clamours of the law courts, desert places, variety of barbarous people, feasts, lamentations, and markets. Take it altogether, it is a strange medley. And yet you will find the diversity of the parts contributes to the harmony of the whole."

49. By looking back into history, and considering the fate and revolutions of government, you will be able to draw a guess, and almost prophesy upon the future; for they will certainly be of the same nature, and cannot but be cast in the same mould. So that forty years of human life may serve for a sample of ten thousand. For what more will you see?

50. "What's sprung from earth dissolves to earth again,
And heaven-born things fly to their native seat."

That is, there is a loosing of the entanglements of the atoms, and a scattering abroad of the insensible elements.

51. "With food, and drinks, and cunning magic arts,
Turning the channel's course to 'scape from death."

"The breeze which heaven has sent
We must endure, and toil without complaint."

52. Can another man ride or fence better than you? It may be so. Let nobody outdo you in social

and modest behaviour. Let nobody be more resigned to fate and forgiving to his neighbours.

53. As long as a man can make use of that reason which he shares with the gods and man, he need not question the event. There can be no grounds to suspect misfortune, provided you stick close to nature and act in accordance with your condition.

54. It is always and everywhere in your power to resign to the gods, to be just to mankind, and to examine every impression with such care that nothing may enter that is not well examined.

55. Never make any rambling enquiries after other people's thoughts, but look directly at the mark which nature has set you. Nature, I say, either that of the universe or your own; the first leads you to submission to Providence, the latter to act as becomes you. Now that which is suitable to the frame and constitution of things is what becomes them. To be more particular, the rest of the world is designed for the service of rational beings in consequence of this general appointment, by which the lower order of things are made for the use of the more noble. And rational creatures are designed for the advantage of each other. Now a social temper is that which human nature was principally intended for; the next thing designed in our being is to be proof against corporeal impressions, it being the peculiar privilege of reason to move within herself, and not suffer sensation or passion to break in upon her; for these are both of animal and inferior quality. But the understanding part claims a right to govern, and will not bend to matter and appetite;

and good reason for it, since she was born to command and make use of them. The third main requisite in a rational being is to secure the assent from rashness and mistake. Let your mind but compass these points, and stick to them, and then she is mistress of everything which belongs to her.

56. We ought to spend the remainder of our life according to nature, as if we were already dead, and had come to the end of our term.

57. Let your fate be your only inclination, for there is nothing more reasonable.

58. When any accident happens, call to mind those who have formerly been under the same circumstances, how full of surprise, complaint, and trouble they were about the matter. And where are they now? They are gone, their murmuring could not make them immortal. To what purpose should you imitate their behaviour? Cannot you leave these foreign emotions to those who cause them, and those who are moved by them? Your business is only to consider how you may give a turn of advantage to the emergency. Now you can make good use of them, and they will supply excellent material, if you will but take care, and do nothing but what is warrantable. Always remembering, that whether you use it ill or well, the thing wherewith action is concerned, is in both cases indifferent.

59. Look inwards, for you have a lasting fountain of happiness at home that will always bubble up if you will but dig for it.

60. Take care that your motions and gestures may

be grave and composed, for the same air of sense and decency which the mind can put into the face ought to be visible through the whole body, but then all this must be done without the least affectation.

61. The art of living resembles wrestling more than dancing, for here a man does not know his movement and his measures beforehand. No, he is obliged to stand strong against chance, and secure himself as occasion shall offer.

62. Consider what sort of people are they that must commend you, and how are their understandings furnished. Truly, if you do but consider the source of their opinions and passions, you will pity their ignorant misbehaviour, and not care a rush for their approbation.

63. It is a saying of Plato's, that no soul misses truth of her own good-will. The same may be said with reference to justice, sobriety, good-nature, and the like. Be particularly careful to remember this, for it will help to sweeten your temper towards all men.

64. When you lie under any corporeal affliction, let this thought be at hand to relieve you: that there is no disgrace in pain, that the sovereign part of your mind is never the worse for it. For how can she suffer unless her material or her social nature be impaired? Besides, Epicurus's maxim will help to support you under most pains; for as he observes, they will neither be intolerable nor everlasting. But then you must keep in mind the limits set to them, and not run into the common opinion about them. And here you must remember that there are many more

sensations than we are aware of, which belong to the nature of pain, such as drowsiness, excessive heat, want of appetite. Now, when you find yourself fret and grow disturbed at these things, take notice that pain has got the better of you.

65. Do not return the temper of ill-natured people upon themselves, nor treat them as they do the rest of mankind.

66. Which way are we to conclude that Socrates was a better man in virtue and temper than Telauges? To make out this, it is not enough to say that he disputed better with the sophists, and died more bravely; that he passed the night in the cold with more endurance, and that when he was bidden to arrest Leon of Salamis, he held it nobler to refuse; that he walked with a swaggering air in the streets, though the truth of this last particular may be questioned. To prove the point, we must examine what sort of soul Socrates carried about with him. Could he be contented with the conscience of an honest and a pious man? Did he abstain from fretting and fuming to no purpose at the knavery and wickedness of the age? Was he governed by nobody's ignorance? Did he never question the equity of Providence, grow surprised at his hard fortune, and sink under the weight of it, and not dip his soul too deep in his senses?

67. Nature has not wrought your composition so close that you cannot withdraw within your own limits, and do your own business yourself; for a man may be first-rate in virtue and true value, and yet be very obscure at the same time. You may likewise

observe that happiness has very few wants. Granting your talent will not reach very far into logic, this cannot hinder the freedom of your mind, nor deprive you of the blessings of sobriety, beneficence, and resignation.

68. You may live with all the freedom and satisfaction imaginable, though the whole world should cry you down; nay, though wild beasts should tear this flesh with which you are enveloped. For pray, how can anything of this reach up to your mind and ruffle her serenity? How can it prevent your passing a right judgment upon your circumstances, and making the best use of them? And thus your reason may address the object of terror: "Look you! nature has made you one thing, and common mistake another." And use may address what befalls, "It is you I was seeking." For it is my way to make everything serve as an opportunity for rational or social virtue in a performance of some duty either to God or man. For since all that happens is related to God or man, there is nothing new in it or difficult to deal with, but all is familiar and easy.

69. He that is come to the top of wisdom and practice, spends every day as if it were his last, and is never guilty of over-excitement, sluggishness, or insincerity.

70. Though the gods are immortal, and have their patience tried through so many ages, yet they are not angry, because for so long a time they will have to put up with such base and wretched mortals, but even provide liberally for them. And are you, that are just going off the stage, sick of the company? are

you tired with evil men already, and yet one of those unhappy mortals yourself?

71. It is great folly not to part with your own faults which is possible, but to try instead to escape from other people's faults, which is impossible.

72. Whatever business tends neither to the improvement of your reason, nor the benefit of society, the rational and social faculty thinks beneath it.

73. When you have done a kindness, and your neighbour is the better for it, why need you be so foolish as to look any farther, and gape for reputation and requital?

74. Nobody is ever tired of advantages. Now to act in conformity to the laws of nature is certainly an advantage. Do not you therefore grow weary of doing good offices, whereby you receive the advantage.

75. There was a time when the universal nature moved towards making the world. So that now all events must either be consequences of the first creation, or else even the chief things at which the universal ruling principle aims are without design. Now this thought will go a great way towards making a man easy.

BOOK VIII.

BOOK VIII.

1. TO keep you modest and free from vain glory, remember that it is no longer in your power to spend your life wholly, from youth upwards, in the pursuit of wisdom. Your friends and yourself, too, are sufficiently acquainted how much you fall short of philosophy; you have been liable to disturbance, so that the bare report of being a philosopher is no longer an easy matter for you to compass; you are unqualified by your station. However, since you know how to come at the thing, never be concerned about missing the credit. Be satisfied, therefore, and for the rest of your life let your own rational nature direct you. Mind, then, what she desires, and let nothing foreign disturb you. You are very sensible how much you have rambled after happiness, and failed. Neither learning, nor wealth, nor fame, nor pleasure could ever help you to it. Which way is it to be had then? By acting up to the height of human nature. And how shall a man do this? Why, by getting a right set of principles for impulses and actions. And what principles are those? Such as state and distinguish good and evil. Such as

give us to understand that there is nothing properly good for a man but what promotes the virtues of justice, temperance, fortitude, and independence, nor anything bad for him, but that which carries him off to the contrary vices.

2. At every action ask yourself this question, What will the consequence of this be to me? Am I not likely to repent of it? I shall be dead in a little time, and then all is over with me. If the present undertaking is but suitable to an intelligent and sociable being, and one that has the honour to live by the same rule and reason with God himself; if the case stands thus, all is well, and to what purpose should you look any farther?

3. Alexander, Julius Cæsar, and Pompey, what were they in comparison of Diogenes, Heraclitus, and Socrates? These philosophers looked through things and their causes, and their ruling principles were in accordance. But as for those great princes, what a load of cares were they pestered with, and to how many things were they slaves!

4. People will play the same pranks over and over again, though you should burst.

5. In the first place, keep yourself easy, for all things are governed by the universal nature. Besides, you will quickly go the way of all flesh, as Augustus and Hadrian have done before you. Farther, examine the matter to the bottom, and remember that your business is to be a good man. Therefore, whatever the dignity of human nature requires of you, set about

it at once, without "ifs" or "ands"; and speak always according to your conscience, but let it be done in the terms of good nature and modesty and sincerity.

6. It is the work of Providence to change the face of things, and remove them from one place to another. All conditions are subject to revolution, so that you need not be afraid of anything new, for all things are usual, and equally distributed.

7. Every being is at ease when its powers move regularly and without interruption. Now a rational being is in this prosperous condition when its judgment is gained by nothing but truth and evidence, when its designs are all meant for the advantage of society, when its desires and aversions are confined to objects within its power, when it rests satisfied with the distributions of the universal nature of which it is a part, just as much as a leaf belongs to the nature of the tree that bears it. Only with this difference, that a leaf is part of a nature without sense or reason, and liable to be checked in its operations, whereas a man is a limb as it were of an intelligent, righteous, and irresistible being, that is all wisdom, and assigns matter and form, time, force, and fortune, to everything in one measure and proportion. And this you will easily perceive if you do not compare one thing with another in every detail, but compare the whole of one thing with the whole of another.

8. You have no leisure to read books, what then? You have leisure to check your insolence. It is in your power to be superior to pleasure and pain, to be deaf to the charms of ambition. It is in your power

not only to forbear being angry with people for their folly and ingratitude, but over and above, to cherish their interest, and take care of them.

9. Never again let any man hear you censure a court life, nor seem dissatisfied with your own.

10. Repentance is a reproof of a man's conscience for the neglect of some advantages. Now, whatever is morally good is profitable, and ought to be the concern of a man of probity. But no good man would ever be inwardly troubled for the omission of any pleasure, whence it follows that pleasure is neither profitable nor good.

11. What is this thing considered in itself? Of what sort of substance, of what material and causal parts does it consist? What share of action has it in the world? and how long is it likely to stay there?

12. When you find yourself sleepy in a morning, remember that business and doing service to the world is to act up to nature and live like a man. Whereas sleep you have in common with the beasts. Now those actions which fall in with a man's nature are more suitable and serviceable, yes, and more pleasant than others.

13. Upon every new impression let it be your constant custom to examine the object in the light of physics, ethics, and dialectics.

14. When you are about to converse with any person, make this short speech to yourself: What notions has this man about good and evil? Then if he has such opinions concerning pleasure and pain, and the causes of them, reputation or ignominy, life

or death; if the case stands thus with him, I shall not wonder at his practice, and I shall remember that it is next to impossible he should do otherwise.

15. Would it not be an odd instance of surprise to stare at a fig-tree for bearing figs? Why then should it seem strange to us for the world to act like itself, and produce things pursuant to quality and kind? This is just as foolish as it would be for a physician to wonder at a fever, or a master of a vessel at a cross blast of wind.

16. To retract or mend a fault at the admonition of a friend in no way hurts your liberty, for it is still your own activity which by means of your own impulse and judgment, and by your own mind, makes you see your mistake.

17. Why do you do this, if it is in your power to let it alone? But if you cannot help it, whom do you blame? The atoms or the gods? Either is folly, and therefore we must murmur against nothing. If you can mend the cause, set about it. If not, mend the thing itself. If you cannot do even that, what are you the better for grumbling? Now a man should never do anything to no purpose.

18. Whatever drops out of life is somewhere, for the world loses nothing. If it stays here, it also changes here, and is dissolved into its proper parts, which are elements of the universe and of yourself. And these two change and do not complain.

19. Everything is made for some end. The sun even will say, I have my business assigned, and so

too the celestial deities. But pray, what were you made for? For your pleasure? Common sense will not bear such an answer.

20. Nature pre-ordains the end of everything, no less than its beginning and continuance, as does he that strikes a ball, and what is the ball the better all this while for mounting, or the worse for flying lower, and coming to the ground? What does a bubble get in the swelling or lose in the breaking? The same may be said of a candle.

21. Turn your body the wrong side outwards, and see it as it is, and consider what age and disease will make of you, and consider that both the orator and the hero, the praiser and the praised, will quickly be out of sight, and that we live but in a corner of this little dimension, that men differ in their notions of honour and esteem, and that even the same person is not of the same opinion long together, and, moreover, that the earth is but a point.

22. Mind that which lies before you, whether it be thought, word, or action. You are well enough served for choosing rather to become good to-morrow than be good to-day.

23. Am I about anything? I will do it with regard to the interest of mankind. Does anything happen to me? I receive it, referring it to the gods, and the fountain of all things whence springs all that happens.

24. Think a little, and tell me what you meet with in the business of bathing? There is oil and sweat, and dirtiness and water, but an offensive mix-

ture, take it altogether. Why, life and everything in it is made up of such indifferent stuff.

25. Lucilla buried Verus, and followed him soon after. Secunda did the same office for Maximus, and survived but a little while. And thus it fared with Epitynchanus and Diotimus, with Antoninus and Faustina, with Celer and the Emperor Hadrianus; they assisted at one funeral, and quickly made another themselves. Where are those men of wit, force, and knowledge, and the others puffed up with pride? They made a great noise and figure formerly, but what is become of them now? Where are those sharp-witted philosophers, Charax, Eudæmon, Demetrius the Platonist, and others of their learning? Alas! they took but a turn in the world, and are gone long since. Some of them have sunk at once, and left no memory behind them. The history of others is overcast, and dwindled into fables, and a third sort have dropped even out of fables. Your business is therefore to remember, that after death this compound of yours will fall to pieces; or else your soul will either be extinguished or removed into another station.

26. Satisfaction consists in doing the things we were made for. And how is this to be compassed? By the practice of general kindness, by neglecting the movements of our senses, by distinguishing appearance from truth, and by contemplating the nature of the universe and its works.

27. Every man has three relations to acquit himself in: his body that encompasses him makes one,

the Divine cause that gives to all men all things another, and his neighbours a third.

28. If pain is an affliction, it must affect either the body or the mind; if the body is hurt, let it say so; as for the soul, it is in her power to preserve her serenity and calm by supposing the accident no evil; for judgment and impulse, aversion and desire, are lodged within, and there no mischief can come at them.

29. Rub out the impressions of fancy on the mind by continually saying to yourself, It is in my power to make my soul free from desire or disturbance. I am likewise able to distinguish the quality of things, and make use of them accordingly. These are all privileges of nature, and ought to be remembered as such.

30. When you speak in the senate or elsewhere, speak suitably and without affectation, and let your discourse be always clear.

31. Augustus' court is buried long since; his empress and daughter, his grand-children and ancestors, his sister and Agrippa, his relations and domestics, physicians and sacrificers, his favourites, such as Arius the philosopher, and Mæcenas, they are all gone. Go on from single persons to families, that of the Pompeys, for instance, and you will find the whole line extinct. "This man was the last of his house," is not uncommon upon a monument. How solicitous were the ancestors of such people about an heir; and yet some one must of necessity be the last. Here, too, consider the death of a whole race.

32. Guide your life towards a single course of action and if every action goes its due length, as far as may be, rest contented. Now, no mortal can hinder you from putting your affairs in this condition. But may not some obstacle from without interpose? No; not so far as to prevent your acting like a man of probity, moderation, and prudence. But perhaps my activity may be checked in some other way. It is no matter for that. As long as you are easy under the obstruction, and pass on smoothly to whatever offers, you have at once another opportunity for action, in accordance with this aforesaid government.

33. As to the case of good fortune, take it without pride, and resign it without reluctance.

34. If you have observed a hand or a foot cut off, and removed from the body, just such a thing is that man, as far as lies in his power, who is discontented with fate, and breaks off from the interest of mankind, or who by a selfish act has cut himself off from the union of nature, for by nature he is a part of the whole. But here lies the good luck of the case. It is in your power to set the limb on again. This favour is allowed by God to no other part of the creation that what is separated and cut off should be joined on again. Consider, then, the particular bounty of God to man in this privilege. He has set him above the necessity of breaking off from nature and Providence at all; but supposing he has broken away, it is in his power to rejoin the body, and grow together again, and recover the advantage of being the same member he was at first.

35. Whence come all the powers and prerogatives of rational beings? From the soul of the universe. Amongst other faculties, they have this which I am going to mention. For as the universal nature overrules all mutinous accidents, brings them under the laws of fate, and makes them part of itself, so it is the power of man to make something out of every hindrance, and turn it to his own advantage.

36. Do not take your whole life into your head at a time, nor burden yourself with the weight of the future, nor form an image of all probable misfortunes. This method will but confound you. On the contrary, your way is upon every emergency to put this question to yourself, "What intolerable circumstance is there in all this?" For you will be ashamed to assign particulars, and confess yourself conquered. Besides, you are to remember, that neither what is past nor what is to come need afflict you, for you have only to deal with the present. Now, this is strangely lessened, if you take it singly and by itself. Chide your fancy, therefore, if it offers to shrink for a moment and grow faint under so slender a trial.

37. Do Panthea and Pergamus still wait at the tomb of Verus, or Chabrias and Diotimus at that of Hadrian? That would be absurd indeed! And what if they were there, would those princes be sensible of the service? Granting they were, what satisfaction would it be to them? And suppose they were pleased, would these waiters be immortal? Are they not doomed to age and death with the rest of mankind? And when they are dead, what would the royal ghosts

do for want of their attendance? Alas! all this ceremony must end at last in stench and dust.

38. If you are so quick at discerning, says one, discern and judge wisely.

39. I find no mortal virtue which contradicts and combats justice; this cannot be affirmed of pleasure, for here temperance comes in with a restraint.

40. It is opinion which gives being to misfortune, do not fancy yourself hurt, and nothing can touch you. But what is this "you?" It is your reason. But I am not all reason. Very well, but do not let reason grow uneasy. And if any other part of you is in trouble, let it keep its concerns to itself.

41. To be checked in the functions of sense, and motion, and desire is an evil to the animal life; that which hinders the growth or flourishing of a vegetable may be said to be an evil there, so likewise to be cramped in the faculties of the mind is an evil to an intelligent nature. Apply all this to yourself. Does pleasure or pain attack you? Turn them over to your senses, and let them answer for it. Does anything cross your undertaking? Why, if you are positive and peremptory about it, the disappointment is really an evil to your rational nature. But if you consider the usual course of things, then no manner of hindrance or harm has happened to you; indeed, no mortal can put a restraint upon the soul; and neither fire nor sword, slander, tongue, nor tyrant can touch her; just as a sphere when it has once come into being remains a sphere.

42. Why should I vex myself that never willingly vexed anybody?

43. Every man has his particular inclination, but my pleasure lies in a sound understanding, a temper that never falls out either with men or accidents, that sees and takes all things with good humour, and puts them to the uses they are fit for.

44. Make the best of your time while you have it. Those who are so solicitous about fame never consider that future generations will be much the same as the present whom they are vexed with, and they, too, are mortal, what then can the noise or opinions of such little mortals signify to you?

45. Toss me into what climate or state you please, for all that, I will keep my divine part content, if it can but exist, and act in accordance with its nature. What! is this misadventure big enough to ruffle my mind and make it deteriorate? To make it mean, craving, and servile, and frightened; what is there that can justify such disorders?

46. No accident can happen to any man but what is consequent to his nature. And the same thing may be affirmed of a beast, a vine, or a stone. Now if things fare no otherwise than according to kind and constitution, why should you complain? You may be assured the universal nature has never laid upon you an intolerable evil.

47. If anything external vexes you, take notice that it is not the thing which disturbs you, but your notion about it, which notion you may dismiss at once if you please. But if the condition of your mind

displease you, who should hinder you from rectifying your opinion? Farther, if you are disturbed because you are not active in the discharge of your duty, your way is rather to do something than to grieve at your own omission. But you are under some insuperable difficulty; then never vex yourself about the matter, for you have nothing to answer for. It may be you will say: It is not worth my while to live unless this business can be effected. Why then, even die; but take your leave contentedly, go off as smoothly as if you were in full activity, and be not angry with those that disappointed you.

48. The mind is invincible when she turns to herself, and relies upon her own courage; in this case there is no forcing her will, though she has nothing but obstinacy for her defence. What then must her strength be when she is fortified with reason, and engages upon thought and deliberation? A soul unembarrassed with passion is a very citadel, the most impregnable security for man in future; hither we may retire and defy our enemies. He that has not seen this advantage must be ignorant, and he that neglects to use it unhappy.

49. Do not make more of things than your senses report. For instance, you are told that such an one has spoken ill of you. Right; but that you are really the worse for it is no part of the news. Again, I see my child lie sick. True; but that he is in danger is more than I see. Thus always stop at the first representation, and add nothing yourself from within, and you are safe. Or rather, reason upon it like a

man that has looked through the world, and is no stranger to anything that can happen.

50. Does your cucumber taste bitter? Let it alone. Are there brambles in your way? Avoid them then. Thus far you are well. But, then, do not ask what does the world with such things as this, for a natural philosopher would laugh at you. This expostulation is just as wise as it would be to find fault with a carpenter for having saw-dust, or a tailor shreds in his shop. Yet they have places where to bestow these. But universal nature has no place for refuse out of herself, but the wondrous part of her art is that though she is circumscribed, yet everything within her that seems to grow old and moulder and be good for nothing, she melts down into herself and recoins in another figure, and thus she neither wants any foreign substance or by-place to throw the dross in, but is always abundantly furnished with room, and matter, and art within herself.

51. Be not heavy in business, nor disturbed in conversation, nor rambling in your thoughts. Keep your mind from running adrift, from sudden surprise and transports, and do not overset yourself with too much employment. Do men curse you? Do they threaten to kill and quarter you? How can this prevent you from keeping your mind pure, wise, temperate, and just? It is much as if a man that stands by a pure and lovely spring should fall a-railing at it, the water never ceases bubbling up for all that; and if you should throw in dirt or clay, it would quickly disappear and disperse, and the fountain will

not be polluted. Which way now are you to go to work, to keep your springs always running, that they may never stagnate into a pool? I will tell you: you must always preserve in yourself the virtues of freedom, of sincerity, sobriety, and good nature.

52. He that is unacquainted with the nature of the world, must be at a loss to know where he is. And he that cannot tell the ends he was made for, is ignorant both of himself and the world too. And he that is uninstructed in either of these two points, will never be able to know the design of his being. What do you think then of his discretion, that is anxious about what is said of him, and values either the praise or the censure of those folks that know neither where they are, nor who?

53. What! Are you so ambitious of a man's good word, that curses himself thrice every hour? Are you so fond of being in their favour, that cannot keep in their own? And how can they be said to please themselves, who repent of almost everything they do?

54. Let your soul work in harmony with the universal intelligence, as your breath does with the air. This correspondence is very practicable, for the intelligent power lies as open and pervious to your mind, as the air you breathe does to your lungs, if you can but draw it in.

55. Wickedness generally does no harm to the universe, so too in particular subjects, it does no harm to any one. It is only a plague to him in whose power it lies to be rid of it whenever he pleases.

56. My will is as much my own as my constitu-

tion; and no more concerned in the will of another man, than my breath and body is in another man's. For though we are born for the service of each other, yet our liberty is independent. Otherwise my neighbour's fault might be my misfortune. But God has prevented this consequence, lest it should be in another's power to make me unhappy.

57. The sun is diffused, and bestows itself everywhere, but this seeming expense never exhausts it. The reason is, because it is stretched like a thread, and thus its beams have their name from extension. As for the properties and philosophy of a ray, you may observe them, if you like to let it into a dark room through a narrow passage. Here you will see it move in a straight line, till it is broken, and, as it were, divided, by having its progress stopped by a solid body; and here the light makes a stand, without dropping or sliding off. Thus you should let your sense shine out and diffuse, extended but not exhausted; and when you meet with opposition, never strike violently against it, nor yet drop your talent in despair: But let your beams be fixed, and enlighten where they find a capacity. And as for that body that will not transmit the light, it will but darken itself by its resistance.

58. He that dreads death is either afraid that his senses will be extinguished or altered. Now, if you have no faculties, you will have no feeling. But if you have new perceptions, you will be another creature, and will not cease to live.

59. Men are born to be serviceable to one another, therefore either reform the world or bear with it.

60. Understanding does not always drive onward like an arrow. The mind sometimes by making a halt, and going round for advice, moves straight on none the less, and hits the mark.

71. Look nicely into the thoughts of every one, and give them the same freedom as your own.

BOOK IX.

BOOK IX.

1. INJUSTICE is no less than high treason against heaven. For since the nature of the universe has made rational creatures for mutual service and support, but never to do anybody any harm, since the case stands thus: he that crosses upon this design is profane, and outrages the most ancient Deity; so, too, does the liar outrage the same Deity. For the nature of the universe is the cause of all that exists. Thus all things are one family united, and, as it were, of kin to each other. This nature is also styled truth, as being the basis of first principles and certainty. He, therefore, that tells a lie knowingly, is an irreligious wretch, for by deceiving his neighbour he is unjust to him. And he that is guilty of an untruth out of ignorance is liable to the same charge, because he dissents from the nature of the whole, brings disorder into the world, and opposes the nature of the universe. Yes, and he opposes himself too, who is borne to what is at variance with truth. By neglecting the impulses he was born to, he has lost the test of truth, and the distinction of right and wrong. Further, he that reckons prosperity and pleasure among things

really good, pain and hardship amongst things really evil, can be no pious person; for such a man will be sure to complain of the administrations of Providence, and charge it with mismatching fortune and merit. He will often see evil people furnished with materials for pleasure, and regaled with the relish of it, and good men harassed and depressed, and meeting with nothing but misfortune. Now, he that is afraid of pain will be afraid of something that will always be in the world; but this is a failure in reverence and respect. On the other hand, he that is violent in the pursuit of pleasure, will not hesitate to turn villain for the purchase. And is not this plainly an ungodly act? To set the matter right, where the allowance of God is equally clear, as it is with regard to prosperity and adversity (for had He not approved both these conditions, He would never have made them both), I say, where the good liking of heaven is equally clear, ours ought to be so too, because we ought to follow the guidance of nature and the sense of the Deity. That man, therefore, that does not comply with Providence in the same indifference with respect to pleasure and pain, life and death, honour and infamy, he that does not this without struggling of passions, without unmanageable preference or aversion, is no friend to the Divine government.

By saying that universal nature or God stands equally affected to these different dispensations, the meaning is that they are both comprehended in the general scheme, and equally consequent to the first establishment. They were decreed by Providence from the beginning, and struck out with the lines of the creation. Then it was that the plan of providence was drawn, and the fate of futurity determined. Then nature was made prolific, and enabled to bring forth in due time. Then the whole stock of beings, the revolutions of fortune, and the successions of time, were all stated and set going.

2. He is better bred and more a gentleman, that takes leave of the world without a blot on his scutcheon, and has nothing of falsehood and dissimulation, of luxury or pride, to tarnish his character. But when a man is once dipt in these vices, the next best thing is for him to quit life. Have you determined to abide with vice, and has not even experience yet taught you to fly from the plague? For the destruction of the understanding is a far worse plague than the corruption and change of the air that surrounds us; for the brute only suffers in the first case, but the man in the other.

3. Do not despise death, but accept it willingly; look upon it as part of the product of nature, and one of those things which providence has been pleased to order. For such as are youth and age, growth and manhood, down and gray hairs, pregnancy and birth, and all natural actions, and incidents of life, so also is dying. A wise man, therefore, must neither run giddily nor impatiently and contemptuously into his grave. He must look upon death as nature's business, and wait her leisure as he does for the progress and maturity of other things; for as you wait for a child to come into the world when it is

ready, so you should stay in the other case till things are ripe, and your soul drops out of the husk of her own accord. But if you stand in need of a vulgar remedy to soothe the mind, consider, then, what sort of world and what sort of customs you will be rid of! It is true you are not to fall foul upon mankind, but to treat them with kindness and gentleness. But still you may remember that you will not be leaving men just of your own mind and fancy. Such a unanimity amongst mortals might reasonably recommend life, and make us loth to part with it. But you perceive that vast disturbances are bred by different opinions; insomuch that now we ought rather to petition death to make haste, for fear we too should forget our true selves.

4. He that commits a fault abroad is a trespasser at home; and he that injures his neighbour, hurts himself, for to make himself an evil man is a great mischief.

5. Omissions no less than commissions are oftentimes part of injustice.

6. If your judgment pronounces rightly, if your actions are friendly and well meant, if your mind is resigned to all that proceeds from the external cause at this moment; if you are in possession of these blessings, you are happy enough.

7. Do not be imposed on by appearances; check your impulses, and moderate your desire, and keep your reason always in her own power.

8. The souls of brutes are all of one kind, and so are those of rational beings, though of a rational kind.

And thus all living creatures that have occasion for air, and earth, and light, are furnished with the same kind, all that have the faculty of vision and life.

9. Things of the same common quality have a tendency to their kind. Earthy bodies fall to the ground. One drop of moisture runs after another; and thus air, where it is predominant, presses after air, and nothing but force and violence can keep these things asunder. Fire, likewise, mounts upwards on account of its own element, fire, but it has such a disposition to propagate its species and join every other fire here below, that it catches easily upon all fuel a little more dry than ordinary, because in such the qualities opposite to ignition are weak and disabled. Thus all beings which partake of the same common intelligent nature have a natural instinct for correspondence with their own kind; only with this difference, that the higher anything stands in the scale of being, the more it is inclined to communication with its own order. To illustrate the argument, we find the force of nature very active amongst brute animals, as appears by their running together in herds and swarms according to kind; by their providing for their young ones, and by that resemblance of love which is carried on among them. These animals have a soul in them, by consequence their principle of union is more vigorous than in plants, stones, and wood. To go on to reasonable creatures, we may observe them united by public counsels and commonwealths, by particular friendships and families, and in times of war they have truces

and treaties. Farther, to instance a higher order, the stars, though not neighbours in situation, move by concert. Thus where things are more noble and nature rises, sympathy rises too, and operates even among distant objects. But now see what happens. The rational creatures are the only beings which have now forgotten this mutual desire and inclination, and here alone this flowing together is not seen. But though they run from their kind, they are brought back again in some measure. For great is the power of nature, and you shall sooner see a piece of earth refuse to lie by its own element, than find any man so perfectly unsociable as not to correspond with somebody or other.

10. God and men and the world all of them bear fruit in their proper seasons. It is true, use has restrained this signification to vines and trees; but this custom apart, reason may properly enough be said to bear fruit for itself and for the common good, especially if we consider that the fruit of the understanding keeps close to its kind and resembles the stock.

11. Give an injurious person good advice, and reform him if you can. If not, remember that your good temper was given you for this trial; that the gods too are so patient as even to pass by the perverseness of such persons, and sometimes to assist them over and above in their health, fame, and fortune; so benign are they. Just thus may you do if you please; if not, where is the impediment?

12. Do not drudge like a galley slave, nor do business in such a laborious manner as if you had a mind

to be pitied or wondered at; but desire one thing only, to move or halt as social reason shall direct you.

13. To-day I rushed clear out of all misfortune, or rather I threw misfortune from me; for to speak truth, it was not outside, nor ever any farther off than my own fancy.

14. All things are the same over again, and nothing but what has been known to experience. They are momentary in their lasting, and coarse in their matter, and all things are now as they were in the times of those we have buried.

15. Things stand without doors and keep their distance, and neither know nor report any things about themselves. What is it, then, that pronounces upon them? Nothing but your own ruling principle.

16. As the good and evil of a rational, social animal consist in action and not in feeling, so it is not what they feel but what they do, which makes mankind either happy or miserable.

17. It is all one to a stone whether it is thrown upwards or downwards; it is no harm for it to descend, or good for it to mount.

18. Examine into men's understandings, and you will see what sort of judges even of themselves are those whom you fear.

19. All things are in a perpetual flux and a sort of consumption; you yourself are continually changing, and in a manner destroyed, and the whole world keeps you company.

20. Let everybody's fault lie at his own door.

21. The intermission of action, and a stop in appe-

tite and opinion, and even a kind of death upon the faculties, is no harm. Go on now to the different periods of life, and here you will find infancy, youth, manhood, and old age, and one, as it were, the death of another. And where lies the terror of all this? Proceed to your life in your grandfather's time, and to that in your father's and mother's, and run over as much ground in differences, changes, and decay as you please, and ask yourself what grievance there is in this, and you may conclude that ending and cessation and alteration of your whole life will be no worse.

22. Hasten to examine your own ruling principle, and that of the universe, and that of your neighbour. Your own, that you may keep it honest; that of the universe, that you may know what you are part of; your neighbour's, that you may discover whether he acts through ignorance or with knowledge; and here you should likewise remember that you are of kin to him.

23. As you are a member of society yourself, so every action of yours should tend to the benefit and improvement of it. So that when you do anything which has neither immediate nor remote reference to general advantage, you make a breach in your life, destroy its unity, and are as really guilty of seditious behaviour as a malcontent in an assembly, as far as in him lies, disturbs the general harmony.

24. Children's anger, mere baubles, wretched souls, bearing up dead bodies, so that the picture of the underworld makes a more vivid impression.

25. Penetrate the quality of forms, and take a

view of them, abstracted from their matter; and when you have done this, compute the common period of their duration.

26. You have been a great sufferer for not being contented with your guiding principle, when it does what it was made for. But enough!

27. When people treat you ill, blame your conduct, or report anything to your disadvantage, enter into the very soul of them; examine their understandings, and see of what nature they are. You will be fully convinced that the opinion of such mortals is not worth one troublesome thought. However, you must be kind to them, for nature has made them your relations. Besides, the gods give them all sort of countenance, warn them by dreams and prophecy, and help them to those things they have a mind to.

28. The periodic movements of the universe are the same up and down from age to age. This uncertain world is always rolling, and turning things topsy-turvy. Now the soul of the universe either pursues its course towards each particular, in which case accept what it brings with it; or else it only moved to create at first, and all things followed one another by necessary consequence. But if neither of these hypotheses will satisfy, you must set Epicurus's atoms at the helm. In a word, if God governs, all is well; but if things are left to themselves, and set adrift, do not you float at random with them. We shall quickly be all underground; and ere long the earth itself must be changed into something else,

and that something into another form, and so on to infinity. Now he that considers these everlasting alterations, this constant tossing and tumbling, and how fast revolutions succeed each other, he will have but a mean opinion of what the world can afford.

29. The universal cause runs rapid like a torrent, and sweeps all things along. What wretched statesmen are those counterfeits in virtue and philosophy! Mere empty froth! Hark you, friend! let honesty be served first. Do what nature requires of you. Fall on, then, as occasion offers, and never look about for commendation. However, I would not have you expect Plato's Republic. As the world goes, a moderate reformation is a great point, and therefore rest contented; for who can change men's opinions! And yet unless you can change their opinions, their subjection will be all force and dissembling. Come now! tell me of Alexander, Philip, and Demetrius of Phalerum. Men shall see whether they had a right notion of the laws of nature, and whether they educated themselves. If they acted like tragedy heroes, no one has condemned me to imitate them. Philosophy is a modest and simple profession, do not entice me to insolence and pride.

30. Fly your fancy into the clouds, and from this imaginary height take a view of mortals here below. What countless herds of men and countless solemnities! What infinite variety of voyages in storm and calm! What differences in the things that become, exist with us, and perish! Go on with the speculation, stretch your thoughts over different aspects of the past and the future, and the present among barbarous nations; how many are there that never heard your name, how many that will quickly forget you, and how many that admire you now will censure you afterwards? In short, memory and fame, and all those things which are commonly so much valued, are of no account at all.

31. Keep a calm spirit towards things that proceed from an external cause, and a just spirit towards those that proceed from a cause within you; that is, let your impulse and action aim at the interest of mankind, for then you know your faculties are in the right posture that nature has set them.

32. The greater part of your trouble lies in your fancy, and therefore you may free yourself from it when you please. I will tell you which way you may move much more freely, and give yourself elbow-room. Take the whole world into your contemplation, and consider its eternal duration, and the swift change of every single thing in it. Consider how near the end of all things lies to their beginning! But then the ages before our birth and after our death are both infinite and immeasurable.

33. Whatever you see now will quickly decay and disappear, and those that gaze upon the ruins of time will be buried under them. And then the longest and the shortest liver will be both in the same condition.

34. If you would look within people, and discover the objects they aim at, and their motives for liking and respect, you must strip them to the soul if you

can. When they fancy that by commending or censuring they do you a good or an ill turn, what a strange conceit it is!

35. Loss is nothing else than change. Things are changed this way, it is true, but they do not perish. Providence, by which all things are well contrived, delights in these alterations. It has always been so in the world, and always will be. What then? Will you say that all things were made ill by so many gods, and must they always remain ill and lack order? And is nature indeed condemned to an everlasting misfortune?

36. The materials of bodies, if you examine them, are strangely coarse; those that are animated have little in them but water, and dust, and bones, and something that is offensive. And again, marble is no more than a callous excrescence of the earth, nor gold and silver any better than its dregs and sediment. Fine cloths are nothing but hair twisted together. Purple is but the blood of a little fish. And thus I might proceed farther. And as for spirits, they are somewhat of kin to the rest, and are chased from one figure to another.

37. Come! you have had enough of life, and grumbling, and apishness; what makes you disturbed? What can you be surprised at? What has happened to you worse than you had reason to expect? Does cause or matter make you uneasy? Look into them, and you may probably be relieved. Now for your comfort, besides these two natures, there is no other. It is high time therefore to become

simple and behave better towards the gods. Three years' time to peruse these things is as good as a hundred.

38. If such a man has done amiss, the mischief is to himself; and it may be, if you inquire, he has not done it.

39. Either all things proceed from one intelligent source, who makes the world but one whole; and if so, why should a part or single member complain of that which is designed for the benefit of the whole? Or else we are under the misrule of atoms, and confusion, and dispersion. Why then do you trouble yourself. Say to your ruling faculty, "You have passed through death and corruption, and forms of animals; and even now you are playing a part, herding and feeding with the rest."

40. Either the gods have power to assist us, or they have not. If they have not, what does praying to them help you? If they have, why do you not rather pray that they would remove your fears and moderate your desires, and rather keep you from grieving for any of these things, than keep away one thing and grant another? For if the gods can help us, no doubt they can help us to be wiser. But it may be you will say, they have put this in my power. Why, then, do you not make use of your talent, and act like a man of spirit, and not run cringing and creeping after that which is out of your reach? But then who told you that the gods do not assist us in things which we might possibly compass by ourselves? Begin, then, to pray for such things, and you will see. For instance,

this man prays that he may gain such a woman, but do you rather pray that you may have no such inclination. Another invokes the gods to set him free from some trouble; but let it be your petition that your mind may never put you upon such a wish. A third is very devout to prevent the loss of his son; but I would have you pray rather against the fear of losing him. Let this be the rule for your devotions, and see if the event does not answer.

41. "When I was sick," says Epicurus, "I did not discourse to my visitors about my diseases, or the torment I was troubled with. No, my system of natural philosophy was part of my subject; and my main concern was, that my mind, although it partakes in these disturbances of the body, should remain calm, and maintain its own good. I gave no handle to the doctors to brag of their profession and what they did for me, but held on with fortitude and indifference." And when you are sick, or under any other disadvantage, cannot you behave yourself as he did? It is practicable to all persuasions in philosophy to stand their ground against all accidents, and not to join in all the foolish talk of the ignorant, who are unacquainted with nature. We must always be prepared, mind the thing at present before us, and the tools, too, with which we are to work.

42. When you are shocked by any man's impudence, put this question to yourself: "Is it possible for such impudent people not to be in the world?" No, indeed. Why, then, do you demand an impossibility? For this ill-behaved fellow is one of those

necessary rascals that the world cannot dispense with. This reflection will furnish you with patience for a knave, a faithless person, or any other evil body. For when you consider that there is no living without such men, you will treat them better individually; and to fortify you further, consider what an antidote nature has given you against this disease. For supposing you have to do with a troublesome blockhead, you have meekness and temper given you for your guard, and so with the rest. It is likewise in your power to inform the man better, and set him right; for everyone that does an ill action is really out of his way, and misses his mark, though he may not know it. Besides, what harm have you received? If you examine the case, you will find none of these provoking mortals have done your mind any damage. Now that is the place in which what is evil and harmful to you originates. Pray, where is the wonder if an ignorant fellow acts ignorantly? If you expected other things from him, you are much to blame. Your reason might make you conclude that he would misbehave in this way, and yet, when that which was most likely has happened, you seem surprised at it. But especially if you accuse any man of ingratitude and infidelity, the fault is your own, if you believed that a man of this disposition would keep faith, or else in conferring a favour you did not give absolutely, for otherwise you would have been satisfied with a generous action, and made virtue her own reward. You have obliged a man, it is very well. What would you have more? You have acted according to your own nature, and must you still have a reward over and above? This is just as if an eye or a foot should demand a salary for their service, and not see or move without something for their pains. For as these organs are contrived for particular functions, in performing which they pursue their nature and attain their perfection, so man is made to be kind and oblige. And, therefore, when he does a good office, and proves serviceable to the world, he has fulfilled the end of his being, and attains his own reward.

BOOK X.

BOOK X.

1. O MY soul, are you ever to be rightly good, simple, and uniform, unmasked, and made more visible to yourself than the body that hangs about you? Are you ever likely to relish good nature and general kindness as you ought? Will you ever be fully satisfied, get above want and wishing, and never desire to seek your pleasure in anything foreign, either living or inanimate? Not desiring, I say, either time for longer enjoyment nor place for elbow-room, nor climate for good air, nor the music of good company? Can you be contented with your present condition, and be pleased with all that is about you, and be persuaded that you are fully furnished, that all things are well with you; for the gods are at the head of the administration, and they will approve of nothing but what is for the best, and tends to the security and advantage of that good, righteous, beautiful, and perfect being which generates and supports and surrounds all things, and embraces those things which decay, that other resembling beings may be made out of them? In a word, are you ever likely to be so happily qualified as to converse with the gods

and men in such a manner as neither to complain of them nor be condemned by them?

2. Examine what your nature requires, so far as you have no other law to govern you. And when you have looked into her inclinations never balk them, unless your animal nature is likely to be worse for it. Then you are to examine what your animal nature demands; and here you may indulge your appetite as far as you please, provided your rational nature does not suffer by the liberty. Now, your rational nature admits of nothing but what is serviceable to the rest of mankind. Keep to these rules, and you will regard nothing else.

3. Whatever happens, either you have strength to bear it, or you have not. If you have, exert your nature, and never murmur at the matter. But if the weight is too heavy for you, do not complain; it will crush you, and then destroy itself. And here you are to remember that to think a thing tolerable and endurable is the way to make it so if you do but press it strongly on the grounds of interest or duty.

4. Is anyone mistaken? Undeceive him civilly, and show him his oversight. But if you cannot convince him, blame yourself, or not even yourself.

5. Whatever happens to you was pre-ordained your lot from the first; and that chain of causes which constitutes fate, tied your person and the event together from all eternity.

6. Whether atoms or nature rule the world I lay it down in the first place, that I am part of that

whole which is all under nature's government. Secondly, I am in some measure related to those beings which are of my own order and species. These points being agreed, I shall apply them. Insomuch then as I am a part of the universe, I shall never be displeased with the general appointment; for that can never be prejudicial to the part which is serviceable to the whole, since the universe contains nothing but what is serviceable to it. For the nature of no being is an enemy to itself. But the world has this advantage above other particular beings, that there is no foreign power to force it to produce anything hurtful to itself. Since, therefore, I am a member of so magnificent a body, I shall freely acquiesce in whatever happens to me. Farther, inasmuch as I have a particular relation to my own species, I will never do anything against the common interest. On the other hand, I shall make it my business to oblige mankind, direct my whole life for the advantage of the public, and avoid the contrary. And by holding to this conduct, I must be happy, as that citizen must needs be who is always working for the benefit of his fellow-citizens, and perfectly satisfied with that interest and station the government assigns him.

7. All the parts of the whole that lie within the compass of the universe must of necessity corrupt and decay; by corruption I mean only alteration. Now if this be an evil and a necessary one, by consequence the whole of nature must be in a bad condition, by having the parts so slenderly put together, and so very liable to destruction. And if the case stands thus,

nature must either design unkindness to the parts of her own body, by making them subject to unavoidable evil in doing or receiving, or else have these things come about without her knowledge. But both these suppositions are highly improbable. Now if any man has a mind to drop the term Nature, and affirm that these things are naturally produced, he that affirms this does but expose himself, by granting in the first place that the parts of the universe are made for alteration, and then wondering and complaining, as if such accidents were unnatural and extraordinary, especially since things do but return whence they came, and are dissolved into their first principles. For either the elements are scattered at large, or else that which is solid turns to earth, and the particles of air join their own element; and thus they are received into the rational substance of the universe, which will either be destroyed by fire after a certain period, or else be renewed by perpetual vicissitudes. Now I would not have you think that those particles of earth or air which you have now in your constitution are the same with those you brought into the world with you. The matter which now belongs to you is as it were but of yesterday's growth or of the day before, and you have taken it all in by food, or the air you breathe, and therefore the alterations in your body do not rob you of the flesh and blood you had from your mother, but only of some later additions. But suppose the same body you were born with is so closely connected with that other, this is no objection to the former statement.

8. When you have given yourself the titles of a man of goodness and modesty, of truth and prudence, of resignation and magnanimity, take care that your practice answers to your character, and if any of these glorious names are lost in your mismanagement, recover them as soon as you can: remembering withal, that prudence implies consideration, care, and discriminating enquiry; that to be resigned signifies a cheerful compliance with the allotments of universal nature; that magnanimity imports a superiority of the reasoning part to the pleasure and pain of the body to glory and death, and all those things which people are either fond or afraid of. Now if you can deserve the honour of these names, do not desire them from other folks; you will be quite another man, and will enter into a new life, and indeed it is high time to begin; for to desire to go on at this rate, to be polluted with appetite, and harassed with passion any longer, is a senseless and a scandalous wish. It resembles the meanness of those poor wretches in the amphitheatre, who when they are half devoured, and have nothing but wounds left them, beg notwithstanding to be respited till the morrow; though they know they will only be thrown again to the same claws and teeth that tore them before. Work into the soul of you these few names of credit, and if you find you can abide by them, stand your ground, and think yourself transported to the fortunate islands. But if you perceive that you are overmatched, and begin to give way, retire cheerfully into some quiet nook, where you may manage better. And if this

will not do, you may give life the slip, but do this without anger. Walk simply, gravely, and freely into the other world, and thus the last action of your life will be the only one worth the owning. And to remember those good qualities above mentioned the more effectually, you should remember the gods, and that they had much rather that all rational natures should resemble than flatter them, that trees are distinguished by their fruit, dogs and bees by the qualities proper to their kind, and men too by the appellation of mankind.

9. Plays, warfare, terror, torpor, servility, will daily wear away these holy principles of yours, which in your study of nature you hastily conceive and let go again. Upon all occasions you should look and act in such a manner as to omit neither the perfect performance of business nor the activity of thinking, to be modest in the consciousness of your improvement, but not so far as to undervalue your knowledge, and keep it out of sight. When will you relish simplicity? when gravity? When will you be able to understand everything, to pronounce upon its nature and its place in the universe; to calculate its continuance, and the ingredients it is made up of, who are likely to be affected by it, and what powers they are which can both give and take it away?

10. A spider when it has caught a fly thinks it has done some great deed, and so does a sportsman when he has run down a hare, and a fisherman too when he has caught a sprat in a net. Some others

must kill boars or bears before they can grow conceited; and a fourth sort value themselves upon hunting Sarmatians; though it may be in this last case, if you go to the definition of robbing, the one are as much thieves as the other.

11. Observe the steps, and continually study the history of nature, and trace the progress of bodies from one form and species to another; contemplate often upon this subject, for there is nothing contributes so much to greatness of mind. He that is rightly affected with this speculation has in a manner laid his body aside. He considers that this world will quickly be over with him, that he must take his leave of mankind and everything here. In consequence of these thoughts, he is all justice in his acts, and resignation in all else. And as for what people will say or think of him, or practise against him, he never minds it. He has but two points to secure—that is, to be honest in what he now does, and contented with what he now receives. As for other projects and fancies, he has done with them. His business is only to follow that straight path which law has chalked out for him, for in so doing he has the Deity for his guide.

12. Why need you be anxious about the event when you may examine the enterprise, and debate the reasonableness of it? If you find it practicable, go on contented, and let nothing divert you. But if you cannot see your way, make a halt, and take the best advice upon the case. And if you happen to be stopped by some new emergency, make the most of what is in your power with due consideration, and

always stick to what appears just; for after all, that is the best thing to get. For though the grand design may not succeed, yet your failure arose from attempting this. The man who follows reason in all things is calm, and yet easily moved, cheerful, and yet grave.

13. When you are first awake you may put this question: whether another man's virtue will signify anything to you in doing your business? No, it will signify nothing. And do not forget what sort of men those are which value themselves so much upon the good or ill character they give their neighbours. How scandalously do they live? How are they overgrown with luxury and vice? How foolish are their fancies, and how unreasonable their fears? See how they steal and rob, not with hands and feet, but with their most valuable part, which, if a man pleases, can produce fidelity, modesty, truth, law, happiness.

14. He that is truly disciplined and reverent will address nature in this language: "Give me what you please, and take what you please away." And there is not the least tincture of vanity in this, but it proceeds wholly from obedience and satisfaction with her.

15. Your time is almost over, therefore live as if you were on a mountain. Place signifies nothing, if you live everywhere in the world as in a social community. Never run into a hole, and shun company. No. Let the world see and recognise in you an honest man who lives according to nature; and if they do not like him, let them kill him, for it is much better he were served so, than to live as they do.

16. Spend no more time in stating the qualifications of a man of virtue, but endeavour to get them.

17. Take the whole bulk of matter and all the extent of time frequently into your thoughts. And then consider that all particular bodies are but a grain in the proportion of substance, and but the turning a gimlet in respect of time.

18. Examine all things closely, and you will find them already decaying and changing, and, as it were, rotting or dispersing, or else things are made as it were to be unmade again.

19. Consider what an humble figure people make when they are eating or sleeping. But then when they put on lordly airs, and strut about, or grow angry, and abuse their inferiors from an altitude! And yet how many little masters did they lately cringe to, how mean was their salary, and what a sorry condition will they come to in a short time?

20. That is best for every man which universal nature sends him; and the time of sending too is also a circumstance of advantage.

21. The earth, as the poet has it, loves the refreshment of a shower, and the lofty ether loves the earth. And the world loves to execute the decrees of fate; and therefore, say I to the universe, your inclinations and mine shall always be the same. And do we not often say: This loves to be produced?

22. Either you will take the benefit of custom, and continue to live, or you cut yourself off from the world; and this, too, was your wish; or you cease to live, then

death will give you your discharge. One of these cases must happen, therefore be not discouraged.

23. Take it for a rule that this piece of land is like any other, and that all things here are the same as on the top of a mountain, or by the sea-shore, or where you will. In this case, as Plato observes, the walls of a town and the inclosure of a sheepfold may be much the same thing.

24. How does my guiding principle stand affected? To what condition am I now bringing it, and to what uses do I put it? Does thought run low with me? Am I grown selfish, and broken loose from the general interest? Is my soul as it were melted and mingled with the body, and perfectly governed by it?

25. He that runs away from his master is a fugitive; now the law is every man's master, and therefore he that transgresses it is a deserter. And all those that are dissatisfied, angry, and uneasy, desire that something past, present, or future should not be, of that which was appointed by the ruler of all, which is justice, and which gives every one his due, and break through the orders of Providence. Thus he who is dissatisfied, or angry, or uneasy, is a deserter.

26. A man deposits seed in a womb, and then another cause takes it and works on it, and makes a child. What a thing from such a material! Again the child passes food down its throat, and again another cause takes it, and makes perception and motion, life and strength, and other things, both many and strange! Observe then the things that are thus produced in darkness, and recognise the power just as

we perceive the power which carries things upwards and downwards, not with the eyes, but no less plainly.

27. You will do well to remember that the world is just as it was formerly, and will go on at the same rate. If you either dip into history, or recollect your own experience, you will perceive the scenes of life strangely uniform, and nothing but the old plays revived. Take a view of the courts of Hadrian, Antoninus Pius, of Philip, of Alexander, or Crœsus, and you will find the entertainment the same, only the actors are different.

28. He that struggles with his fortune, and makes an affliction of it, is much like a pig that kicks and cries out when his throat is cutting; and he that, when he is sick, mourns to himself over the bonds in which we are held, is not much better. We should consider that none but rational creatures have the privilege of making necessity a choice; merely to submit is what all are compelled to do.

29. Consider the satisfactions of life singly, and examine them as they come up, and then ask yourself if death is so terrible in taking them from you.

30. When anybody's misbehaviour disturbs you, immediately turn to yourself and bethink you whether you have not been guilty of the same fault; for instance, whether you have not over-valued money, or pleasure, or fame, or the like. Such reflections will quickly make you forget your anger, especially if you consider that the offender was not altogether his own man, but under some untoward compulsion. For

what else could he do? Therefore, if you can, step in to the rescue and free him from the compulsion.

31. When you consider Satyrion the Socratic, think upon Eutyches or Hymen; and when you remember Euphrates, think upon Eutychion or Sylvanus; and when Alciphron comes into your head, carry your thoughts to Tropæophorus; and when you are musing upon Xenophon, let Crito or Severus come into the contemplation; and when you make yourself the subject of your meditations, bring some of the emperors, your predecessors, into your company; and thus set the dead and the living of the same character and profession always one against another; then ask the question: Where are those men? The answer will be: They are nowhere, or at least nowhere that I know of. Thus you will be strongly convinced that men are but smoke and bubbles; and this impression will go the deeper if you consider that what is once perished and sunk will never come up again throughout the ages. As for your share of time, it is but a moment in comparison. Why then cannot you manage that little well and be satisfied? What a noble opportunity of improvement do you run away from? For what are all the revolutions of nature, and the accidents of life, but trials of skill and exercises of reason that has looked through the causes of things carefully and philosophically. Go on then till you have digested all this and conquered the difficulty, for I would have you be like a strong stomach, that masters all sort of diet, and makes nourishment of it; or if you please, like a fire well kindled, which catches at everything you throw in, and turns it into flame and brightness.

32. Put it out of the power of any one truly to report you not to be a sincere or a good man; let your practice give him the lie; this is all very feasible, for pray who can hinder you from being just and sincere? To make all sure, you should resolve to live no longer than you can live honestly; for, in earnest, reason would rather you were nothing than a knave.

33. What is it that is most proper to be said or done upon the present occasion? Let it be what it will, I am sure it is in your power to perform it, and therefore never pretend it impracticable. You will never leave grumbling till you can practise virtue with a relish, and make it your pleasure to perform those acts that are suited to the constitution of a human being; for a man ought to hold it a pleasure to do everything that is suitable to his nature, and that is in his power. Now this is in his power everywhere. The motion of a cylinder may be stopped, fire and water may be checked in their tendency, and so may any part of the vegetable and animal world. In this case a great many obstructions may interpose, but there is nothing can block up a soul, stop the course of reason, or hinder a thought from running in its natural channel as it pleases. He that considers the irresistible liberty of the mind, that she moves as easily as fire does upwards, as a stone downwards, as a cylinder on a smooth descent, seeks nothing farther; for all other impediments proceed either from the body, which is really a corpse, or else they are founded

in opinion, and unless we betray ourselves, and desert our reason, can do us no manner of mischief; otherwise, ill fortune, as it is commonly called, would make a man ill, for all other productions of nature or art, when any harm happens to them, are certainly the worse for it, but here a man is, so to speak, the better for what he suffers; he improves his value and raises his character by making a right use of a rugged accident. In short, I would have you remember, that no citizen can receive any damage by that which does not affect the community, neither can the community suffer unless the laws suffer too; but these misfortunes, as they are called, do not violate the laws, therefore they do not hurt the community, nor by consequence the citizen.

34. He that is well tinctured with philosophy needs but a short receipt, a common cordial will keep up such a man's spirits and expel fear from his heart. For instance—

> "As leaves on trees the race of man is found,
> Now green in youth, now withering on the ground."

So your children are but leaves. Leaves, too, are the echoes of praise, and censure, and silent blame, and reproach. Leaves, too, are the continuance of fame. All these matters, like leaves, have their spring for growing, then a puff of wind sends them packing, and quickly after the wood is new furnished again. Things are strangely short-lived, and yet you fear and pursue them as if all were everlasting, but for all that, you will soon close your eyes, and then he that is your chief mourner will quickly want another for himself.

35. An eye that is strong and rightly disposed is indifferent to all colours, therefore if it calls for green, it is a sign it is weak and out of order. Thus when the hearing and smelling are in good condition, they do not pick and choose their objects, but take in all manner of scents and sounds. Thus a strong stomach despatches all that comes into it, like a mill that grinds all sorts of grain. And thus a mind that is sound and healthy is prepared to digest all sorts of accidents, and therefore when it is clamorous in such wishes as these: "O that my children may live and flourish, that I may be commended for everything I do!" when the mind, I say, is thus sickly, it is just like an eye that is all for green colours, and like a set of teeth that would touch nothing by their good will but soft things.

36. There is nobody so happy in his family and friends, but that some of them when they see him going will rejoice at his death. Let him be a person of probity and prudence, somebody or other will drop some of these sentences over his grave. "Well! our man of order and gravity is gone, we shall now be no more troubled with his discipline! I cannot say he was ill-natured to any of us, but for all that, I am sensible he condemned us in his heart." This is the best treatment a good man must expect. But alas! as for our conduct, how many reasons will people muster up to be rid of us! If you consider this when you are dying, you will quit life with the less reluctance. Say then to yourself, "I am leaving an odd sort of world, where the sharers in my fortune, and the

objects of my care and kindness, those people for whom I have drudged and contrived, and wished so heartily, count my life no better than a grievance, and would fain be rid of me; now who would be fond of staying in such company any longer?" However, this thought must not go so deep as to sour your humour. You must keep your temper, and part friendly with every body, but then your good nature must not make you hang back. For as when a man has an easy death, the soul slides gently out of the body, so you must walk off handsomely, and bid the world adieu without regret. It is true, nature has twisted your interests, and tied you together, but now she loosens the knot, and makes the sign to disengage. I will part then with the world as with my friends and relations, but for all my kindness I will not be dragged from them but go of my free will. For this too is ordained by nature.

37. Let it be your constant method to look into the design of people's actions, and see what they would be at, as often as it is practicable; and to make this custom the more significant, practise it first upon yourself.

38. Remember that what pulls and hales you from one passion to another, is but your fancy within you. There lies the rhetoric that persuades you. That is the live thing, and to speak plainly, that is the man, after all. But when you talk of a man, I would not have you tack flesh and blood to the notion, nor those limbs neither which are made out of it. These are but tools for the soul to work with. Now the only

difference is that nature has glued them as it were to the soul, but the use of them depends solely upon the mind. It is the will that either checks or sets them going. They have but the force of instruments, and signify no more without foreign direction, than a shuttle, a pen, or a whip, which will neither weave, nor write, nor lash the horses, without somebody to manage them.

BOOK XI.

BOOK XI.

1. THE properties of a rational soul are these. She has the privilege to look into her own nature, to cut out her qualities and form herself to what character she pleases. She enjoys her product (whereas trees and cattle bring plenty for other folks). Whether life proves long or short, she gains the ends of living. Her business is never spoilt by interruption, as it happens in a dance or a play. In every part and in spite of every interruption, her acts are always finished and entire; so that she may say: I carry off all that belongs to me. Farther, she ranges through the whole world, views its figure, looks into the vacuum on the outside of it, and strains her sight on to an immeasurable length of time. She contemplates the grand revolutions of nature, and the destruction and renewal of the universe at certain periods. She considers that there will be nothing new for posterity to gaze at; and that our ancestors stood upon the same level for observation; in so much that in forty years' time a tolerable genius for sense and enquiry may acquaint himself with all that is past and all that is to come by reason of the uniformity of all things.

Lastly, it is the property of a rational soul to love her neighbours, to be remarkable for truth and sobriety, to prefer nothing to her own dignity and authority, which has likewise the custom and prerogative of a law; and thus far right reason and rational justice are the same.

2. The way to despise the pleasure of a fine song, a well-performed dance, or the athletic exercises, is as follows: as for the song, take the music in pieces and examine the notes by themselves, and ask as you go along, "Is it this or this single sound, that has subdued me?" You will be ashamed to confess the conquest. Thus, to lessen the diversion of dancing, consider every movement and gesture apart; and this method will hold with respect to athletic contests. In short, all things but virtue and virtuous acts abate by taking them asunder, and, therefore, apply the expedient to all other parts of your life.

3. What a brave soul is that that is always prepared to leave the body and unconcerned about her being either extinguished, scattered, or removed—prepared, I say, upon judgment, and not out of mere obstinacy like the Christians—but with a solemn air of gravity and consideration, and in a way to persuade another and without tragic show.

4. Have I obliged anybody, or done the world any service? If so, the action has rewarded me. This answer will encourage good nature, therefore let it always be at hand.

5. What may your trade or profession be? It is to live like a man of virtue and probity. And how

can this end be compassed, but by the contemplation of the nature of the world and of mankind in particular.

6. As to dramatic performances, tragedy appeared first. The design of them was to show that the misfortunes of life were customary and common, and that what attracted them upon the stage, might surprise them the less when they met with it on the larger stage of the world. Thus people see that these events must happen, and that even those who cry out, "*O Cithaeron*," cannot stand clear of them. And to give the stage-poets their due, they have some serviceable passages, as, for instance,

> "If I and mine are by the gods neglected,
> There's reason for their rigour."

Again—

> "Ne'er fret at accidents, for things are sullen,
> And don't regard your anger;"

Once more—

> "Fate mows down life like corn, this mortal falls,
> Another stands a while."

And others like them. Next to tragedy, old comedy took a turn upon the stage; and here pride and ambition were lashed and pointed at with great freedom and authority, and not without some success; and for this reason, Diogenes sometimes borrowed from them. You are now to observe that middle comedy succeeded to the old, and the new to the middle, this last kind sinking by degrees to the buffoonery of the mimi. It is true, there are some useful expressions to be met with even here; but then you are to consider the tendency of the whole poetic art, and whether these dramatic diversions drive at any aim.

7. Nothing is clearer to me than that the present state of your life is as good for philosophy and improvement as any other whatsoever.

8. A bough by being lopped off from another, must of necessity be lopped from the whole tree; thus a man that breaks with another loses the benefit of the whole community. It is true a bough is lopped off by a foreign hand, but the man pulls himself asunder by his untoward aversion and hatred to his neighbour. He little thinks how he disincorporates himself by this unhappy division from the body of mankind! And here the goodness of God who founded this society is extraordinary. He has put it in our power to grow to the limb we left, and come again into the advantage of the main body. But if this misfortune is often repeated, it will be a hard matter to restore the part and close the division. For, as gardeners observe, a bough cut off and grafted in again is not in the same good condition with another which always flourished upon the trunk. We should be one in growth, though not in sympathy.

9. People's malice or impertinence cannot beat you off your reason, or stop your progress in virtue. Be not then disconcerted, nor check your good nature towards them. If you meet with opposition and ill-will, you must neither be diverted nor disturbed, but keep your right judgment and action and your temper

too towards people who try to hinder you or otherwise annoy you. For as it is a weakness to give in from fear and be diverted from your conduct, so it is likewise to be angry with impertinent people. They are both a sort of deserters from Providence, who are either frightened from their duty, or fall out with those of their own nature and family.

10. Nature falls short of art in no instance, art being but an imitation of nature; and if so, the most perfect and all-embracing nature cannot be supposed to work with less skill than a common artificer. Now, in all arts the less in value are contrived for the sake of the greater. This, therefore, is the method of universal nature, and upon this ground justice is founded. The other virtues are but acts of justice differently applied. But just we can never be if we are eager and anxious about external advantages, if we are apt to be led astray and grow over-hasty, and inconstant in our motion.

11. Aversions and desires are the general occasions of disturbance. Now since the objects of these passions do not press upon you, but it is you that make up to them in some measure, you should let your opinion about them lie still, and they too will keep still, and then you will neither be seen pursuing nor avoiding them any longer.

12. The figure of the soul is then round and uniform, when she neither reaches after anything foreign, nor shrinks into herself, nor is dispersed or sunk in, but shines in the light by which she surveys the truth of all things and of herself too.

13. Does anyone despise me? It is his look-out. I will take care not to give him any reason for his contempt by my words and acts. Does anyone hate me? It is his look-out. I will continue kind and good-humoured to all the world, even to the injurious person himself. I am always ready to show him his error without abuse, or making a display of my own patience, but frankly, and with cordial sincerity, as Phocion did, unless indeed this was put on. Indeed your mind should always be so disposed, that the gods may examine you, and perceive that you are neither angry nor uneasy at anything. Now, if you follow the current of your nature of your own free will, and accept that which is now suitable to the universal nature, where is the harm in it, when you know you were made on purpose to comply with the interest of the universe?

14. People generally despise where they flatter, and cringe to those they would gladly overtop.

15. How fulsome and hollow does that man look that cries, "I'm resolved to deal straightforwardly with you." Hark you, friend, what need of all this flourish? Let your actions speak; your face ought to vouch for your speech. I would have virtue look out of the eye, no less apparently than love does in the sight of the beloved. I would have honesty and sincerity so incorporated with the constitution, that it should be discoverable by the senses, and as easily distinguished as a strong breath, so that a man must be forced to find it out whether he would or no. But on the other side an affectation of sincerity is a very dagger. Nothing

is more scandalous than false friendship, and, therefore, of all things avoid it. In short, a man of integrity, sincerity, and good-nature can never be concealed, for his character is wrought into his countenance.

16. To bestow no more upon objects than they deserve; and where things are indifferent, to let our thoughts be so too, is a noble expedient for happiness, and this faculty we have in our souls. The way to attain to this indifference is to look through matters, and take them quite asunder, remembering always that things cannot enter into the soul, nor force upon us any opinions about them; they are quiet. It is our fancy that makes opinions about them; it is we that write within ourselves, though it is in our power not to write. And if any false colours are laid on by surprise, we may rub them out if we please. We are likewise to consider that this trouble will not last, that death will relieve us soon. Where, then, is the difficulty of standing upon our guard a little while? If these things are in accordance with nature, bid them heartily welcome, and then your inclination will make you easy; but if they prove contrary to nature, look out for something that is more serviceable to your nature, and pursue that, even if it bring you no glory. For certainly every man may make himself happy if he can.

17. Consider the original of all things, the matter they are made of, the alterations they must run through, and the result of the change. And that all this does no manner of harm.

18. Concerning those that offend, consider in the first place, the relation you stand in towards men, and that we are all made for each other. And for my own part I am particularly set at the head of the world, like a ram over a flock, or a bull over a herd. You may go higher in your reasoning, if you please, and consider that either atoms or nature governs the universe. If the latter, then the coarser parts of the creation were made for the service of their betters; and these last for the sake of each other.

Secondly. Consider what men are at bed and board, and at other times; especially you should remember what strong compulsion of opinion they lie under, and with what pride they perform their acts.

Thirdly. Consider that if those men are in the right, you have no reason to be angry; but if they are in the wrong, it is because they know no better. They are under the necessity of their own ignorance. For as no soul is voluntarily deprived of truth, so nobody would offend against good manners, if they were rightly aware of it. And thus we see people will not endure the charge of injustice, ingratitude, selfishness, or knavery of any description, without being stung at the imputation.

Fourthly. Do not forget you are like the rest of the world, and faulty yourself in a great many instances: that though you may forbear from some errors, it is not for want of inclination, and that nothing but cowardice, vanity, or some such base principle hinders you from sinning.

Fifthly. That it is sometimes a hard matter to be

certain whether men do wrong, for their actions often are done with a reference to circumstances; and one must be thoroughly informed of a great many things before he can be rightly qualified to give judgment in the case.

Sixthly, When you are most angry and vexed remember that human life lasts but a moment, and that we shall all of us very quickly be laid in our graves.

Seventhly, Consider that it is not other people's actions (for they are lodged in their ruling principles), which disturb us, but only our own opinions about them. Do but then dismiss these notions, and do not fancy the thing a grievance, and your passion will have ceased immediately. But how can this fancy be discharged? By considering that bare suffering has no infamy in it. Now unless you restrain the notion of evil to what is disgraceful, you will be under a necessity of doing a great many unwarrantable things, and become a robber and a villain generally.

Eighthly, Consider that our anger and impatience often prove much more mischievous than the things about which we are angry or impatient.

Ninthly, That gentleness is invincible, provided it is of the right stamp, without anything of hypocrisy or malice. This is the way to disarm the most insolent, if you continue kind and unmoved under ill usage, if you strike in with the right opportunity for advice. If when he is going to do you an ill turn you endeavour to recover his understanding, and retrieve his temper by such language as this: I pray you, child, be quiet, men were never made to worry one another. I shall not be injured, but you are injuring yourself, child. Then proceed to illustrate the point by general and inoffensive arguments. Show him that it is not the custom of bees to spend their stings upon their own kind, nor of cattle whose nature it is to dwell in herds. And let all this be done out of mere love and kindness, without any irony or scorn. Do not seem to lecture him or court the audience for commendation, but discourse him either alone, and if others are present, as if there was nobody but himself.

Lay up these nine heads in your memory with as much care as if they were a present from the nine muses, for now it is high time to begin to be a man for your lifetime. And here you must guard against flattery, as well as anger, for these are both unsocial qualities, and do a great deal of mischief. Remember always, when you are angry, that rage is the mark of an unmanly disposition. Mildness and temper are not only more human, but more masculine too. One thus affected appears much more brave, and firm, and manly than one that is vexed and angry. For he that has the least passion in these cases has always the most strength. On the other hand, as grief is a sign of weakness, so is anger too. A man is wounded in both these passions, and the smart is too big for him.

As you have received these nine precepts from the Muses, take this tenth if you please, from their leader, Apollo: That to wish that ill people may not do ill things is to wish an impossibility, and no better than madness. But then to give them leave to plague other folks, and desire to be privileged yourself, is a foolish and insolent expectation.

19. There are four evil qualities we must be particularly careful to avoid, and pull them up as fast as we find them, and address them as they rise in this fashion. "This fancy," say, "is unnecessary; this rough behaviour destroys society; this phrase I cannot say from my heart. Now this is most absurd, not to speak from your heart." These are three of them; and when you shall reproach yourself for anything, since this degrades the diviner part of you, makes your mind truckle to your body, and your reason to your pleasures, look upon that as the fourth.

20. Those particles of fire and air which are lodged in your body, notwithstanding their tendency to mount, submit to the laws of the universe, and keep the rest of the elements company. Again, the earthy and watery parts in you, though they naturally press downwards, are raised above their level, and stand poised in an unnatural position; thus the elements serve the interest of the world. For when they have been fixed anywhere they keep their post till the signal is given to separate. And is it not then a scandalous thing that your mind should be the only deserter, and grow mutinous about her station, especially when her orders agree with her constitution, and nothing that is unnatural is enjoined? And yet she will not bear the conduct of her own faculties, but runs perfectly counter to humanity. For when a man turns knave or libertine, when he gives way to fears and anger

and fits of the spleen, he does as it were run away from himself and desert his own nature; and further, when his mind complains of his fortune it quits the station in which Providence has placed it; for acquiescence and piety are no less its duty than honesty; for these virtues tend to the common interest, and are rather of greater antiquity and value than justice.

21. He that does not always drive at the same end in his life will never be uniform and of a piece in his conduct. But this hint is too short, unless you describe the quality that we ought principally to aim at. Now as people do not agree in the preferences of the things that in some way seem good to the many, unless in what relates to the common good, so a man ought to propose the benefit of society and the general interest of the world as his main aim. For he that levels at this mark will keep an even hand, and thus be always consistent with himself.

22. Remember the story of the country and the town mouse, and how pitifully the former was frightened and surprised.

23. Socrates used to say the common objects of terror were nothing but bogies, fit only to scare children.

24. The Lacedæmonians, at their public shows, seated strangers under a canopy in the shade, but made their own people take their convenience as they found it.

25. Socrates, being invited to Perdiccas's court, made his excuse:—I dare not come, says he, for fear of being put under an incapacity of returning an

obligation, which I take to be the worst way of destroying a man imaginable.

26. It is a precept of the Ephesian philosophers, that we should always furnish our memory with some eminent example of ancient virtue.

27. The Pythagoreans would have us look up into the sky every morning, to put us in mind of the order and constancy of the heavenly bodies, of the equality and purity of their matter, and how frankly they lie open to observation; for a star never wears a veil.

28. Remember how unconcernedly Socrates wore a sheepskin, when Xanthippe had got his coat on, and ran out with it. And how well he laughed off the matter to his friends, who were strangely out of countenance by seeing him in such a disguise.

29. People do not pretend to teach others to write and read till they have been taught themselves; this rule holds much more of life.

30. Be dumb; slaves have not the privilege of speaking.

31. "And my heart laughed within."

32. "And virtue they will curse, speaking hard words."

33. He is a madman that expects figs on the trees in winter; and he is little better that calls for his children again when they are dead and buried.

34. Epictetus would have a man when he is kissing and caressing his child, say to himself at the same time: To-morrow perhaps you may die and leave me. These are words of ill omen, you will say. That is your mistake; the consequences of mortality and the

course of nature are no ominous things to think on, otherwise it would be an ominous business to cut down a little grass or corn.

35. Grapes are first sour, then ripe, then raisins, these are all no more than bare alterations; not into nothing, but into something which does not appear at present.

36. As Epictetus observes, nobody can rob another of his free will.

37. The same philosopher has taught us the art of managing our assent and movements; that we should have a regard to circumstances; that our inclinations should be generous and benevolent, and proportioned to the merit and dignity of things; that we must keep our desires from being headstrong, and never have an aversion for anything which it is out of our power to hinder.

38. Therefore, as Epictetus observes, the contest is no trifle, but whether we are to live in our wits or out of them.

39. It is a saying of Socrates to some untoward people: "What would you be at? Would you have the soul of a man or of a beast in you? Of a man. Of what sort of men, of those that use their reason, or those that abuse it? Of the first. Why then, continues the philosopher, do not you look out for this privilege? Because we have it already. What makes you then disagree, and fall foul upon each other?"

BOOK XII.

BOOK XII.

ALL those things you drudge, and range so much ground for, you may have at your ease, unless you are afraid of making yourself too happy. Your method to do your business is not to concern yourself about the time past, for that is never to be recovered; to rest the future with Providence, and only stick to the present, and improve that to all the noble purposes of piety and justice. The pious part will be discharged by being contented with your fate; and why should you not, since nature made you for each other? And as to the obligations of justice, you will acquit yourself here, provided you speak truth boldly and above board, and make law and the dignity of things your rule to act by. Wherein you are not to be checked in your progress by the misbehaviour, the ignorance, and impertinent reports of other people, nor yet by the sensations of the body that surrounds you, for the part that suffers must look to that. To go on: If, since your life is almost up, you lay aside all other matters, and only cultivate your mind, and pay a regard to the governing and diviner part of yourself; if you are not at all afraid of losing your life, but only of never beginning to live in accordance with nature, then you will act suitably to your extraction, and deserve to be the offspring of the universe ; then you will be no longer a stranger in your own country, nor be surprised at common accidents ; you will never be dependent on this or that.

2. God sees through the soul of every man as clearly as if it was not wrapped up in matter, nor had anything of the shroud and coarseness of body about it. And God, with his intellectual part alone, touches those beings only that have flowed and proceeded from him. Now, if you would learn to do thus, a great deal of trouble would be saved ; for he that can overlook his body will hardly disturb himself about the clothes he wears, the house he dwells in, about his reputation, or any part of this pomp and magnificence.

3. You consist of three parts—your body, your breath, and your mind. The first two are yours to take care of, but the latter is properly your person. Therefore, if you abstract from the notion of yourself, that is, of your mind, whatever other people either say or do, or whatever you may have said or done yourself formerly, together with all that disturbs you under the consideration of its coming to pass hereafter ; if you throw the necessary motions of your carcass out of the definition, and those of the vortex that whirls about you, and by this means preserve your rational faculties in an independent state of innocence, free from the allotments of fate, holding close and steady to the virtues of justice, truth, and acquiescence ; if I say, you keep your mind separate and

distinguished from the objects of appetite and the events of time, both past and future, and make yourself like Empedocles's world,

> "Round as a ball in joyous rest reposing,"

and concern yourself to live no longer than your real life, that is the present moment; if you do all this, you may move on till death stops you, with credit and in harmony with the deity within you.

4. I have often wondered how it comes to pass that everybody should love themselves best, and yet value their neighbour's opinion about themselves more than their own. Therefore, if any god or eminent instructor should stand at a man's elbow and order him to turn his inside outwards, and publish every thought and fancy as fast as they came into his head, he would not submit so much as to a day's discipline; thus we stand more in awe of our neighbour's judgments than our own.

5. How comes it that since the gods have contrived all things so well, and so much to the benefit of mankind, they should overlook this particular, and suffer men of great virtue and merit, who, by their piety and devotion, were, as it were, in communion with the powers above, and kept always a correspondence with heaven, that they should suffer such men, I say, to be finally extinguished by death, and not give them their being again? Now, if the case stands thus, you may be assured had it been proper, the gods would have ordered it otherwise; for had it been right it would have been possible, and

nature would certainly have brought it forth if it had been natural; therefore from its not being matter of fact, if indeed it is not, you may undoubtedly conclude it ought not to be so. For do not you perceive that in reasoning this point you dispute the administration of providence? Now, if the justice and goodness of the gods were not extraordinary, this liberty would not be allowed, neither would you presume so far if you thought otherwise; but, if they have these perfections, they will never neglect their affairs, nor blemish their world with anything that is unreasonable or unjust.

6. Accustom yourself to master things which you seem to despair of, for, if you observe, the left hand, though, for want of practice, it is insignificant in other business, yet it holds the bridle better than the right because it has been used to it.

7. Consider what death will make of you, both as to body and mind, recollect the shortness of life, the immeasurable extent of time, both past and future, and how slenderly all things are put together.

8. Let it be your method to contemplate spirits apart from the shell they are shut up in, mind the aim of people's actions, examine the value of fame, the force of pain and pleasure, and see what death amounts to, and what reputation, consider upon what account a man grows troublesome to himself, that nobody can be hindered by another, and that everything is opinion.

9. We must manage the precepts of philosophy like those that wrestle and box in the circus, and not like a gladiator; for your fencer if he drops his sword is hewn down immediately, but the other that makes

weapons of his limbs has nothing to do but to keep his hands stirring.

10. Be not satisfied with a superficial view of things, but penetrate into their matter and form, and the end they were made for.

11. What a mighty privilege is a man born to, since it is in his power not to do anything but what God Almighty approves, and to be satisfied with all the distributions of Providence.

12. When things follow from the course of nature, we ought not to blame the gods, for they do no wrong either willingly or against their will, nor yet men, for their misbehaviour is all involuntary. Therefore we must complain of nobody.

13. How unacquainted is that man with the world, and how ridiculous does he appear, that makes a wonder of anything he meets with in this life!

14. Either the order of things is fixed by irrevocable fate, or providence may be worked into compassion, or else the world floats at random without any steerage. Now if nature lies under an immovable necessity, to what purpose should you struggle against it? If the favour of providence is to be gained, qualify yourself for the divine assistance; but if chance and confusion prevail, be you contented that in such a storm you have a governing intelligence within you, and if the waves run too high, let them carry away your body, your breath, and all things else, but there is no necessity your mind should be driven with them.

15. A lamp till it is extinguished holds its light, and shines without interruption, and can you find in

your heart to see your truth, honesty, and sobriety extinguished before you?

16. When you fancy anyone has transgressed, say this to yourself: How do I know it is a fault? And granting it is, it may be his conscience has corrected him, and if so, he has torn his own face. Besides, you are to remember, that to wish an evil man should not do amiss, is just as wise as it would be to desire that a fig-tree should not bear juice in the figs, that children should not squall, nor horses neigh, nor a great many other things act according to the necessity of their condition. Pray, how would you have a man of such an unfortunate disposition behave himself? If you are angry, try to cure him.

17. If it is not seemly never do it, if it is not true, never speak it, for your impulse should always be under your control.

18. Look always nicely into whatever makes an impression upon your mind, distinguishing it into cause and matter; and consider its purpose and design and the period of time, beyond which it is unlikely to continue.

19. Consider, for it is high time, that you have something more divine in you than the mechanism of passion, than the wires of a puppet. What is there now in my soul? Is it fear, or suspicion, or desire? Or anything of this coarse nature?

20. Take care never to do anything without thought, and design, nor for any other end but what may be serviceable to the interest of society.

21. Consider that in a little time you will neither

have place, nor being, that your contemporaries will have the same fate, and the present scene of nature be shut up. For all things are formed by nature to change and turn and drop in pieces, that new ones may be continually made out of them.

22. Remember that all things are opinion, and that it is in your own power to think as you please. Therefore remove the opinion, and then as if you had doubled some dangerous cape, you will have nothing but a steady course, a smooth sea, and a waveless bay to receive you.

23. Every activity that ceases in due time, suffers nothing by breaking off: Neither does the agent receive any harm from this. Thus life, which is nothing but a series and continuation of action, comes to no harm by having a seasonable period put to it: Neither does he who has ended this series in due time sustain any loss. Now nature assigns the term of life; sometimes this period is fixed by particular nature, as it happens when a man dies of old age; but let it come late or early, common nature has certainly a hand in it. And thus the parts of nature changing from one form to another preserve the whole world in perpetual youth and vigour. Now that is always good and reasonable which makes for the service of the universe. From hence it follows that bare dying can be no real evil, seeing there is nothing disgraceful in it, for it is both involuntary with respect to ourselves, and serviceable to the general interest. Therefore, it is certainly a good thing, since it is suitable, and seasonable, and profitable to the universe,

for he that follows the Deity with his motions, and is led by his will to the same ends, is led by God himself.

24. Let these three hints lie ready for service. *First*, As to your own actions let nothing be done rashly nor to no purpose, nor indeed in any other manner than justice itself would have ordered it. And as for external fortune, consider that it is the blind distribution of chance or else the appointment of providence. Now either to murmur against chance or impeach providence is extremely absurd. *Secondly*, Consider what a slight thing man is from his conception till he receives his soul; and from its reception till its loss; consider too the parts of his composition and the state of his dissolution. *Thirdly*, Consider that if you could shoot yourself at pleasure into the sky and thence take a view of human affairs, you would perceive a strange medley of condition, and discover at the same time the air, and ether too, plentifully stocked with inhabitants. And that if you mounted never so often, you would have the old prospect. Alas! things are generally of the same complexion and of the same short continuance too, and yet how strangely we are conceited of them.

25. Discharge opinion and you are safe; and pray who can hinder you from doing it?

26. When you are uneasy upon any account, you have forgotten that all things fall out according to the nature of the universe, and that another man's fault is no concern of yours, that what you reckon grievances is nothing but the old way of the world and will come over again, and is now to be met with in a

thousand places. You have forgotten that all mankind are of kin, for though they may be unallied in flesh and blood, their understandings are all of the same family. You do not remember that every man's soul is a portion of the Deity, and derived from thence, that we have nothing properly our own, but that our children, our bodies, and our breath, are all borrowed from heaven, that opinion governs all, and that it is not possible for any body to live, or lose any more than the present moment. All this you seem to have forgotten.

27. Reflect frequently upon those that have formerly been mightily disturbed with accidents of any kind, that have carried their animosities and feuds to the most flaming excess, that have made the most glorious figure or met with the greatest misfortune, and then ask yourself, Where are they all now? They are vanished like a little smoke, they are nothing but ashes, and a tale, or not even a tale. Recollect likewise everything of this sort, what Fabius Catullinus did at his country seat; Lucius Lupus, in his garden; Stertinius, at Baiæ; Tiberius, at Capreæ; Rufus, at Velia, in short, the overweening importance attached to anything whatsoever; and know that the prize is insignificant, and the play not worth the candle. It is much more becoming a philosopher to stand clear of affectation, to be honest and temperate upon all occasions, and to follow cheerfully wherever the gods lead on, for nothing is more scandalous than a man that is proud of his humility.

28. To those that ask me the reason of my being

so earnest in religious worship, and whether I ever saw any of the gods, or which way I am convinced of the certainty of their existence; in the first place, I answer, that the gods are not invisible. But granting they were, the objection would signify nothing, for I never had a sight of my own soul, and yet I have a great value for it. And thus by my constant experience of the power of the gods I have a proof of their being, and a reason for my veneration.

29. The best provision for a happy life is to dissect everything, view its own nature, and divide it into matter and form. To practise honesty in good earnest, and speak truth from the very soul of you. What remains but to live easy and cheerful, and crowd one good action so close to another that there may not be the least empty space between them.

30. The light of the sun is but one and the same, though it is divided by the interposition of walls and mountains, and abundance of other opaque bodies. There is but one common matter, though it is parcelled out among bodies of different qualities. There is but one sensitive soul too, notwithstanding it is divided among innumerable natures and individual limitations. And lastly, the rational soul, though it seems to be split into distinction, is but one and the same. Now, excepting this last, the other parts above-mentioned, such as breath and matter, though without apprehension, or any common affection to tie them to each other, are yet upheld by an intelligent being, and by that faculty which pushes things of the same nature to the same place; but human under-

standings have a peculiar disposition to union; they stick together by inclination, and nothing can extinguish such sociable thoughts in them.

31. What is it you hanker after? Is it bare existence? or sensation? or motion? or strength, that you may lose it again in decay? What? Is it the privilege of speech, or the power of thinking in general? Is any of this worth desiring? If all these things are trifles, proceed to something that is worth your while, and that is to be governed by reason and the Deity. And yet you cannot be said to value these last-mentioned privileges rightly, if you are disturbed because death must take them from you.

32. What a small part of immeasurable and infinite time falls to the share of a single mortal, and how soon is every one swallowed up in eternity! What a handful of the universal matter goes to the making of a human body, and what a very little of the universal soul too! And on what a narrow clod with respect to the whole earth do you crawl upon! Consider all this, and reckon nothing great, unless it be to act in conformity to your own reason, and to suffer as the universal nature shall appoint you.

33. The great business of a man is to improve his mind, therefore consider how he does this. As for all other things, whether in our power to compass or not, they are no better than lifeless ashes and smoke.

34. We cannot have a more promising notion to set us above the fear of death, than to consider that it has been despised even by that sect who made pleasure and pain the standard of good and evil.

35. He that likes no time so well as the fitting season, he that is indifferent whether he has room for a long progress in reason or not, or whether he has a few or a great many years to view the world in, a person thus qualified will never be afraid of dying.

36. Hark ye friend; you have been a burgher of this great city, what matter though you have lived in it five years or three; if you have observed the laws of the corporation, the length or shortness of the time make no difference. Where is the hardship then if nature, that planted you here, orders your removal? You cannot say you are sent off by a tyrant or unjust judge. No; you quit the stage as fairly as a player does that has his discharge from the master of the revels. But I have only gone through three acts, and not held out to the end of the fifth. You say well; but in life three acts make the play entire. He that ordered the opening of the first scene now gives the sign for shutting up the last; you are neither accountable for one nor the other; therefore retire well satisfied, for He, by whom you are dismissed, is satisfied too.

THE END OF THE TWELVE BOOKS OF THE EMPEROR MARCUS AURELIUS ANTONINUS.

NOTES.

BOOK I.

1. Annius Verus was his grandfather's name.

2, 3. Annius Verus was also his father's name; his mother's was Domitia Calvilla. The Emperor T. Antoninus Pius married the sister of Annius Verus, and was thus by marriage the uncle of Marcus Aurelius Antoninus, whom he adopted.

7, 8. Q. Junius Rusticus and Apollonius of Chalcis were Stoic philosophers.

11. M. Cornelius Fronto was a rhetorician, who had been the Emperor's tutor. Part of Marcus Aurelius' correspondence with Fronto is still extant.

13. Cinna Catulus was a Stoic philosopher.

14. The allusion may be to Claudius Severus, a Stoic philosopher.

15. Claudius Maximus was a Stoic Philosopher.

17. "It is the favour of the gods that I happened to meet with a brother." The Emperor had no brother. If this refers to Lucius Verus, his adopted brother, he certainly does not deserve the praise here bestowed.

BOOK II.

13. "As the poet says."—Pindar, quoted in the "Theaetetus" of Plato.

BOOK IV.

27. The Greek word for Universe and Order is the same, *κόσμος*. Thus the "universe," or "universal order," is contrasted with chaos or disorder.

34. Clotho was one of the Fates. They were three sisters—Clotho, the spinning fate; Lachesis, the one who assigns to man his fate; and Atropos, the sister who cut the thread when a man's destiny was accomplished.

BOOK VII.

35. From Plato's "Republic," Book vi. p. 486.

38. From Euripides' "Bellerophon."

40. From Euripides' "Hypsiple."

42. Aristophanes, "Acharnians," l. 661.

44-45. From Plato's "Apology," p. 28.

46. From Plato's "Gorgias," p. 512.

48. This does not appear to be in any of Plato's extant writings. It has been suggested that it should rather be referred to Pythagoras.

50. From Euripides' "Chrysippus."

51. The first two lines are from Euripides' "Supplices," 1110 1111.

66. "Leon of Salamis." In the year 404 B.C., during the terrible tyranny of "the Thirty" at Athens, Socrates was ordered to assist in unjustly arresting a rich citizen of Salamis, and bringing him to Athens for a trial that was only a mockery of justice. Socrates refused to do this; and he alludes to this in the "Apology." "But when the oligarchy of 'the Thirty' was in power, they sent for me and four others into the rotunda, and bade us bring Leon the Salaminian from Salamis, as they wanted to execute him. That was a specimen of the sort of commands they were always giving with a view to implicating as many as possible in their crimes; and then I showed, not in word only, but in deed, that, if I may be allowed to use such an expression, I cared not a straw for death, and that my sole fear was the fear of doing an unrighteous or unholy thing. For the strong arm of the oppressive power did not frighten me into doing wrong, and when we came out of the rotunda, the other four went to Salamis and fetched Leon, but I went quietly home." (Plato, "Apology," p. 32, trs. by Jowett.)

"That he walked in a swaggering way." This is asserted by Aristophanes in his comedy, the "Clouds," where he ridicules Socrates.

BOOK VIII.

3. Caius is Caius Julius Cæsar.

57. Marcus Aurelius is trying to derive the Greek word for rays ἀκτῖνες from the verb ἐκτείνεσθαι—to be extended. The explanation is obviously impossible. Such bad etymology was common at a time when no real science of words existed.

BOOK IX.

29. In his "Republic," Plato sketches an ideal state in which the institutions and government are to attain perfection.

BOOK X.

6. "The islands of the blest." Homer (Od. iv.) speaks of the Elysian plain at the extremity of the world, "where life is easiest for men. No snow is there, nor yet great storm, nor any rain, but alway ocean sendeth forth the breeze of the shrill west to blow cool on men." (Trs. by Butcher and Lang.) Plutarch identifies the Canaries with this description. After describing their delightful climate, he says, "So that it is generally believed even among the barbarians, that these are the Elysian fields and the seats of the blessed" (Plutarch, "Sertorius").

21. There is a sort of play here on the word φιλεῖ, which means both "loves," and "is wont." The Stoics delighted in these plays on words, and even used the names of the gods in a punning sense.

23. The quotation is from Plato's "Theaetetus," p. 174, but it is curiously applied. In the original the words are used disparagingly. Plato is describing the philosopher, and showing with what contempt he would look on the greatness of a tyrant or king. "Then again he observes that the great man is of necessity as ill-mannered and uneducated as any shepherd, for he has no

leisure, and he is surrounded by a wall which is his mountain-pen." (Jowett's translation.)

31. Crito was a friend of Socrates, and gave his name to one of Plato's dialogues.

34. The quotation is from Homer, "Iliad," vi. 146

BOOK XI.

6. "O Cithaeron." The words occur in one of the choruses in Sophocles' "Œdipus Tyrannus," l. 1089. Œdipus had been exposed as an infant on Mount Cithaeron, in order to avoid the terrible doom prophesied him.

22. The first extant version of the story of the town and the country mouse occurs in Horace's "Satires," ii. 6.

26. The Ephesians are probably the followers of Heraclitus.

BOOK XII.

3. Empedocles of Agrigentum was a philosopher who flourished about 444 B.C. He was the first to establish the number of four elements. These were, he thought, acted on by two moving causes—love (combination), and strife (separation). Originally the four elements were combined in a sphere where love reigned supreme, and all was peace and harmony. Strife, which was originally outside the sphere, gradually forced its way in, and so began the period of change in which we are living. Empedocles wrote an epic describing the origin of the world, and from this the line in the text is a quotation.

34. This section refers to the Epicureans. Their doctrine made the chief good consist in pleasure, but as they believed that only virtue would afford true pleasure, their teaching was really capable of producing noble men. Our modern term "Epicurean" in no way does justice to the teaching of Epicurus and his immediate followers.